Emot

Intelligence

Bible

A Collection of 8 Books in 1 - Emotional Intelligence, Social Anxiety, Dating for Introverts, Public Speaking, Confidence, How to Talk to Anyone, Social Skills and Cognitive Behavioral Therapy

ISBN: 978-1-953149-11-4

Second Paperback Edition: June 2020
First Paperback Edition: September 2019

WANT THE AUDIOBOOK FOR FREE?

We have a **limited** amount of **free** promotional codes for this audiobook.

Here's how it works:

1. **Visit the link below** to see the listing on AudiobookRocket
2. Request a free promo code from us
3. In **30 days** leave an honest, unbiased review on the audiobook.
4. Confirm & notify us on AudiobookRocket that you left a review.
5. Request and enjoy additional audiobooks from other publishers on the site.

https://audiobookrocket.com/audiobooks/1

IF YOU ENJOY THE FREE AUDIOBOOK,

PLEASE HELP US OUT AND **LEAVE A REVIEW**

TABLE OF CONTENTS

Book 1.

Emotional Intelligence

A Guide to Mastering Social Skills, Improve Your Relationships, Skyrocket Your EQ and Self Mastery for Success in Life and Business

INTRODUCTION

The general school of thought to become successful in life, relationships and obtain real wealth was to attend a prestigious university, get good grades, work hard and be blessed with a high intelligence quotient. Most would go as far as to assume that if one were blessed with a high IQ, chances of becoming successful were significantly higher.

Your entire life you have been led to believe that this was the direct pathway to success. But the reality is you have only been exposed to a fraction of the equation because success is the product of many different variables.

However, one of the most crucial determining factors is your ability to not only control your own emotions, but those of other people as well.

Emotional intelligence also known as emotional quotient, is defined as an individual's ability to recognize and control their own and other people's emotions.

This concept can easily be understood by breaking it down to two simple components:

1. Recognizing intentions, emotions, desires and goals you have for yourself as well as goals of others.

2. Handling these said emotions and actions to achieve the most positive outcome for all involved.

Emotional intelligence started to gain traction due to a prestigious author by the name of Daniel Goleman, who published his book "Emotional Intelligence" in 1995. His book popularized the concept of emotional intelligence. Before emotional intelligence came into the forefront of the public eye, intelligence quotient or IQ was considered the single biggest determining factor of assessing an individual's capabilities.

Although this approach theoretically seemed to pan out in a controlled classroom and the world of academia, facing the real world where careers, jobs and business fraught with "crabs in a barrel" stood no chance of survival.

As emotional intelligence grew in popularity, IQ was forced to take a back seat to make room for a novel way to evaluate the likelihood of one's success.

Although theoretically this approach seemed great on paper, navigating the ruthless real world relied on an entirely different skill set than what's traditionally taught in the classroom. It has been shown through time a person's degree doesn't always guarantee or directly correlate with a high paying salary or the creation of a successful and profitable business. The likely outcome is you may be viewed as a potentially better candidate for a job interview than others but that's the extent of it.

With that said, it will take much more than intelligence for someone to succeed in life and business. In fact, a combination of skills such as conversation, social, communication and emotional have been shown to be winning factors for a higher probability of success. Interestingly enough, none of these skills are taught in a classroom, but rather having experiences in situations where social interactions are required. Examples of these are more common than one might think, and valuable lessons are hiding in plain sight; Working as a waiter or bartender, participating in team sports, joining a club, volunteering and even stay in hostels where sleeping quarters and common spaces are shared. These social interactions make room for one to learn how to become increasingly resilient to life's difficulties, work well with others, your ability to deal more effectively with change, handle tough or difficult conversations, quickly build trust with people, as well as a rapport and also become a strong and respected leader.

If you still think that IQ is the determining factor to a person's overall success, I challenge you to look no further than top CEOs of large organizations, successful entrepreneurs, presidents and thought leaders. Some of the most well-known and successful businesses were founded by college dropouts, not Stanford, MIT or Harvard graduates with a Ph.D. I'm willing to wager more than likely not every single person who you look up to and admire for their success and ability to have a well-balanced life are top graduates of a prestigious university. By no means am I saying that intelligence on its own is less important. Nor am I recommending you quit school altogether and walk down a path of studying human psychology. If you are blessed with a naturally high intelligence quotient and cognitive abilities that's wonderful, but as you are now aware it's only a fraction of the success equation. If you can complement your already high cognitive abilities with high emotional intelligence you will have the capability to achieve many incredible things. Just think, tons of CEOs, Fortune 500 company founders, world leaders and wildly successful individuals are high school dropouts... If the key to becoming successful was purely based on intelligence, how would you explain their success?

Now if I were to choose between possessing high emotional intelligence or simply a high IQ, I would without a doubt choose emotional intelligence. I see it as simple as this: A person with a high intelligence and less developed emotional intelligence will struggle and have less of a chance of succeeding in today's real world compared to someone with a highly developed emotional intelligence and average intelligence. When you are able to manage people, understand their emotions, know what makes them "tick", what motivates them and manage their feelings you will be far more successful in life. The name of the game is people management. Humans are emotional not logical by nature and are motivated by emotions. Once you realize this, you are able to maneuver skillfully through life.

Let's say you have a team in which their tasks are very technical and requires special knowledge on a daily basis. As a leader, guiding your team with your experiences and technical knowledge will assist in completing tasks, but what about keeping your team motivated? Understanding which emotions motivate them is the key to keeping them inspired to do their best work, be more productive and motivated. That is emotional intelligence. The best part about this skill is that anyone can learn it, including you. Regardless of the outcome of your genetic lottery or what some may call fate, unlike hereditary intelligence, emotional intelligence can be acquired by having a clear vision, practice and a little motivation.

There are many things which are beyond your control in life, however you do have the power and ability to decide how you react in the face of change and unexpected challenges. The objective of this book is to shed light on the important aspects of emotional intelligence and how you can start using them right now. What you may have once thought was a dream to achieve success can become a reality as we unveil practical techniques to raise your emotional quotient and eventually improve your chances of success.

So, if you're looking for a way to not only harness the best version of you, become successful in the most positive way, and also impact others so they too can achieve greatness, then cultivating this powerful skill of emotional intelligence is of the utmost priority. This book will provide you with exercises you can implement today to develop and train your emotional intelligence quickly. You are the author of your own life, keep reading if you're ready to make the change and live a life of fulfillment.

CHAPTER 1. WHAT IS EMOTIONAL INTELLIGENCE?

Elaine and Jessica are two teachers at a primary school; dealing with troubled children is within their job description. The two of them have to keep a classroom full of children calm enough for the education process to go smoothly but unfortunately, one of the children always ends up throwing a tantrum. In their classroom, Jessica and Elaine both had a child crying after a classmate refused to lend them an item. Bruce was denied a magic pen in Jessica's classroom and Rosie a glitter lined ruler in Elaine's. A situation like this is a great source of frustration and stress for all teachers.

To make Bruce settle down, Jessica believes that discipline is the key and sternly scolds him, showing her displeasure. She then proceeds to give a punishment fitting of Bruce's misbehavior.

Elaine, on the other hand likes to rely on communication. She calmly talks to the upset child, Rosie, soothing her before having a conversation with her to determine what pushed her to act the way she did. After a few words with the child, she finds out that she was envious of her classmate's glittery ruler and wanted to use it as well. When Rosie was denied the item, it made her feel frustrated. Elaine then proceeds to tell her why it is wrong to deal with her feelings by throwing a fit and that it doesn't fix anything. She explains to Rosie that she should accept her classmate's decision and to try to ask again nicely by offering to lend a nice item of her own in exchange.

Jessica is unable to handle young children's negative emotions and while her approach may intimidate the child into a calmer state, it doesn't change much on the long term and it wastes a perfect opportunity to teach the child a valuable lesson.

Elaine, knows that there is a reason for Rosie's behavior. Elaine tries to understand the emotion that triggered the temper tantrum, helping Rosie understand it as well while she is at it. Then, Elaine teaches her how to deal with that emotion. This way, she is dealing with her own problems of a crying child in the process.

In the situation above, both teachers faced the same situation of having an upset child on their hands but dealt with it in very different ways. Elaine was empathetic with Rosie and solved the problem from the roots by helping her face and understand her emotions while Jessica was solely concerned with calming down Bruce enough to continue with her lesson.

This is emotional intelligence in a nutshell. The ability to Identify your emotions and those of the people around you and managing them in a way that is positive and productive.

If you search for the meaning of emotional intelligence in the dictionary, you'll find the following definition or some variation of it: "The capacity to be aware of, control, and express one's emotions, and to handle interpersonal relationships judiciously and empathetically" But, what does that mean?

At first glance, you might think that it sounds very basic. We know what we feel and we can handle our relationships just fine. And sure, you might be someone who is considered emotionally intelligent, but there is also the possibility that you're going about it the wrong way. Let's go back to that definition and go through it slowly.

"The capacity to be aware of ... one's emotions."

This means that you must have the ability to recognize an emotion at the moment they are felt. Most importantly, you can quickly spot a negative emotion and do something about it before you react to it. Identifying the emotion is the first step of dealing with it.

In the practical life, think of those moments you felt very strongly about something. Perhaps, a member of the family pushed your buttons by teasing you. Or maybe a colleague blamed you for a delay that they caused. If you take a moment to think about what you are feeling, you will most likely conclude that it is anger or frustration.

Always take the time to identify the emotion in question. If you can't put your finger on it, try to remember the last time you felt this. Try to think about what triggered that emotion and why it is so intense.

Controlling your emotions

"The capacity to... control ... one's emotions."

Ever heard of anger management? That is one aspect of emotional control that has become quite popular lately as people have started to recognize the importance of emotional intelligence. However, anger is not the only emotion that can be managed. Any negative emotions should be kept under regulation. Let's be honest, sometimes even positive ones are not appropriate in certain situations and should be curbed.

Plausible Scenarios

We have all gone through a situation in which we've just lost it. Maybe you got so mad at your nephew who scattered their logos all over the floor and snapped on them after stepping on one; pain can lead to reactions you didn't know you were capable of!

You were walking through the halls of your company and were startled by the appearance of a colleague when turning around a corner and let out an expletive. You were frightened, the words slipped out of your mouth before you even knew what you were saying!

We are not proud of those moments, but they happen. But know that while you may not be able to control how you feel per se, you still have the ability to control your reaction to those feelings.

When you feel overwhelmed by a certain feeling, stop. Take a moment to identify this feeling. Think about why it impacts you so much. Think of how you were about to react to it and then think of the impact of that reaction on your life. Chances are you won't want to react that way. In fact, most people have expressed regret after a spontaneous reaction.

Actionable Tips

1). *Instead of immediately reacting out of an irrational and emotional behavior, slowly count down from five and take deep breaths in between. This will give you pause and an opportunity to calm down.*

2). *If you are confronted with a situation in which you feel you want to give someone a real good tongue lashing, get out a piece of paper and write everything you wanted to say and then seal it in an envelope. Wait a day and then see how you feel about the situation.*

Expressing your emotions

"The capacity to... express one's emotions."

Though you should control your immediate reaction to your emotions, keeping them bottled up is never a good idea. Instead, express your emotions in a productive way and use them as a source of motivation.

Every emotion can be made useful once you identify it and take the time to think about your reaction to it.

Close your eyes and think back for a moment; there must have been a time in your life when you were told your work was not good enough or that you would never succeed and you thought "Watch me, I will prove you wrong!". See how you used the negativity of being belittled, turned it into spite and used that same emotion as a driver to achieve your goals?

You surely know someone who works well under pressure, if you are not one yourself. You see them procrastinate for a week and then work non-stop the entire weekend and surprisingly they manage to pull it off. While some people might have a breakdown when overcome by stress, those people use it as motivation to get things done.

You can do it as well, channel that emotion and use it as a source of inspiration.

Handling your relationships with others

"...To handle interpersonal relationships judiciously and empathetically"

To manage your relationships with other people, you need two key ingredients. Empathy and social skills. The first allows you to understand the emotion that is overcoming them. The second, lets you navigate your way through helping them manage that emotion.

Empathy

Empathy is the ability to feel, understand and relate to other people's emotions. Being able to put yourself in someone else's shoes and seeing things from their perspective is considered one of the pillars of Emotional Intelligence.

You've seen it before. Someone letting out an "Ouch" when a passerby slips and takes a fall. Someone crying in commiseration with a friend after a painful event has occurred. You must have exhibited empathy towards someone at some point in your life or perhaps been on the receiving end.

While helping people is a great and selfless act, empathizing with someone shows that you're ready to go the extra mile to be there for that person. It shows that you care. It also allows you to identify the emotion they are currently feeling and as mentioned above, that is the first step when dealing with emotions.

To use empathy in your favor, observe the person in question. Try to think of what made them feel the way they do to recognize the emotion and think about your state when you are overcome by the same emotion.

Social skills

Once you have spotted the emotion, it is time to do something about it. These skills are necessary when dealing with another person, no matter the setting. If you want to help, you have to do it gracefully and efficiently. Help that person to use their emotions in their favor and make sure you are doing it smartly. Being too soft or too rough can lead them to lock you out and all your efforts will be in vain.

Social skills are also necessary when dealing with people in settings where you are only required to interact. Good manners, charisma and kindness are all key characteristics of leaders and those who are popular, respected and sought after. It's no secret if you want to become popular, practicing these qualities can lead you on the right path.

EQ ABILITY MODEL

To many experts, Emotional intelligence is ability-based. That means that your emotional intelligence is determined by your ability to perceive emotions, use emotions, understand emotions and manage emotions.

This set of skills will allow you to measure your EQ and determine the areas where you are lacking in order to improve.

Perceiving emotions

In the definition of Emotional intelligence, we spoke about being aware of emotions. You can perceive emotions in yourself through your own physical state, feelings and thoughts, while to perceive emotions in other people, you can rely on language, facial expressions, vocal tone and body language.

Try to pay attention to these pointers to determine the corresponding emotion.

Using emotions:

It is the ability to use your emotions and those of others to your advantage. We spoke about using your emotions as a source of motivation, but how about others'? Think of the time you wanted to ask something of your parents and waited until they were well rested and in a good mood to make your request. Get it yet? You used their positive emotions to your advantage because you knew that it was more likely to get you what you want.

Understanding emotions:

The process of understanding emotions goes from identifying the emotion to understanding the reasoning behind that emotion, meaning what lead to its occurrence then to the potential reaction to that emotion.

Understanding an emotion helps you take the proper measures to deal with it.

Managing Emotions:

And this includes controlling your emotions. Responding to them properly and responding to other people's emotions.

While the EQ ability model is slightly different from the definition used above, you can see that it is very similar and shares the key aspects.

Chapter 2. Raising Your Emotional Intelligence

According to experts, EQ accounts for half of your success in life. Some claim that it is even more important than IQ and, in a world, where most activities are wrapped in human interaction, this is no surprise, which is precisely why raising emotional intelligence is necessary.

"How to raise emotional intelligence?" you may ask...

To raise your EQ, you have to work on a few aspects.

Raising self-awareness:

Being self-aware will result in strength of character and integrity. Those are traits that people find highly desirable and believe to make a person trust-worthy.

To raise your self-awareness, be objective and honest with yourself when you try to evaluate yourself. Stay open to the idea that you are only a human being who can make mistakes and who always has the ability to improve. Always try to see your flaws or better put, areas you could improve on. If you find this difficult to self-analyze, simply ask others to honestly point them out for you. It may be a bit challenging for you to notice your flaws, but it is critical for your progress in the long term. Self-awareness also helps you get to know yourself as a person; your likes, dislikes and it can be a way to help put an end to bad habits you may have formed over the years. The beautiful thing about this is that it is like "cleaning house" for your mental clarity. Think of it as out with the old and in with the new. After putting priority on developing the qualities you would ultimately like to exude and making a conscious decision to drop bad habits, you will have a firmer grasp on the things that are most important in your life.

Actionable Tip

1. *Journaling will help you keep track of what you have discovered about yourself. It is very easy to ignore your thoughts, which is why putting them on paper provides you a clear way to keep track of your behavior. Making adjustments when necessary, things are always clearer in hindsight.*

2. *As emotions arise take note of your physiological reactions. Is your heart beating faster than normal? A more heightened sense of focus? Perhaps a sudden sweat has come over you.*

Start to label your emotions to determine what actions are associated with these emotions. When you start to feel an emotion overcoming you, make an honest effort to identify it and what the root cause of it is. Are you feeling anger, anxiety, depression, fear, surprise or perhaps a combination of these?

On the piece of paper draw a line down the middle to create two columns. At the top on the left side put “Emotions” and on the right put “Trigger”. Now you can log each emotion that may arise and the trigger that caused it. You will soon have a list of triggers that made you feel positive or destructive emotions, things that make you feel angry or happy.

For example, have you ever felt jealousy before? I’m sure you have. This may have been evoked because you felt someone was more successful than you are. Putting these on paper will pave the way for you to significantly raise your emotional self-awareness.

Perhaps you even have felt an unnerving dismay for a person, but have no particular reason why. This person has a beautiful family, all of the flashy material things you desire, but a humble and respectful character. The feeling you discover is irrational jealousy. Instead of loathing this person for the life they lead, feel happy for them. The reality is that person is human and more than likely has gone through a fair amount of struggles themselves to achieve what they have in life.

In any given day as humans we are afforded the blessing of experiencing a spectrum of emotions. It’s what makes us feel alive. It’s what makes us human.

Knowing this information is beneficial because after labeling each emotion, you can also harness the power to manage these emotions.

That being said, the only way you can optimize and develop your emotional intelligence is when you are more aware of your own feelings.

Actionable Tip!

Recognize key areas of development that need improvement

- As stated above, get feedback from friends, family and those who you trust and interact with
- Make a list of all of your strengths and weaknesses
- Take a certified, psychological personality assessment test to unveil more of your abilities, limitations, values and skills

Become an Expert on Yourself

Once you are able to identify your own emotions, recognizing emotions and feelings of others will come much more naturally to you. If you ultimately want to bring about change in your behavior, thoughts and actions you absolutely need to understand what needs to be improved on.

The key to becoming emotionally savvy and aware is Knowing yourself inside and out.

FUN FACT!

Were you aware that many athletes are trained to recognize and overcome feelings before an important upcoming game? This is based on the premise that if you can successfully recognize and manage your emotions, it will not impact your productivity.

Close your eyes and think of all the recent times where you let emotions get the best of you, ultimately affecting your productivity. There must have been times when you let trivial matters negatively impact your performance, right? By being aware of your strengths and weaknesses, it is easier to accomplish your goals. There is less of an opportunity for unwanted emotional distractions such as frustration and disappointment in your life which invites lower productivity.

After becoming more in tune with your emotions, you'll also start to notice that these emotions are not singular in nature, but rather multi-dimensional.

For example, you may have had an argument with your significant other in which you felt vengeful, hurt, angry and upset all at the same time. This is quite common as you begin to peel back the layers of the emotions like an onion.

Realize that change doesn't just happen overnight and will take some time to make head way. However, what's most important is that you are taking the initiative to the best version of you.

Raising empathy:

Some people may be natural empaths, but that doesn't mean that empathy cannot be learned. In fact, those natural empaths may not be as "natural" as you are led to believe, they have probably started learning and practicing empathy at a very young age.

To raise your empathy, you need to make interacting with people a top priority. Take the time to listen to them and make sure that they can speak without any interruptions. Some people have trouble expressing themselves and so, it may take more time for them to communicate their thoughts. Do not show signs of boredom like spacing out or checking the time and instead, look at them and show them that you are following what they are saying. Simple nodding in agreement and encouraging them to keep talking can help them put their guard down and open up with their feelings.

Try to find it in yourself to care about their concerns, even if they are different from yours. Think of how you would feel if you were in their place and if you had to deal with their struggles.

Try to help however you can, most times they just need someone to listen to them unload their burdens and you won't need to do much but if you can pitch in to make life easier for them, do it.

Raising self-management and social skills:

These two aspects need practice. Though it might be uncomfortable for you, try to get in as many social interactions as possible. Participate in conversations and if possible, take a friend with good social skills with you to observe you and give you feedback on how you performed. Try to stay aware of your reactions. Once you have the necessary feedback, work on improving yourself by learning where you went wrong and then put yourself to the test by diving back into social interactions with your newly polished social skills and self-regulation.

These situations will force you to increase your self-confidence, which is a key component to developing your social skills. Another great way to improve your confidence is to practice being assertive while you express your thoughts and opinions.

A truly emotionally aware person refuses to become a prisoner of his or her emotions, but rather leverages them to achieve a desired and positive outcome.

Chapter 3. Early Childhood Emotional Intelligence

Most parents are convinced that a high IQ is sufficient for their children's success in life and will lead them to a successful adulthood. The fact is, EQ cannot be neglected and if taught since childhood, it will lead to a better integration with their peers and they can focus on sharpening their academic knowledge.

A crucial time

Early childhood is defined as the period of time that extends from birth to the age of eight. It is considered as a time of incredible growth as the child learns from their surroundings and the people around them. It is also at that time that the development of feelings starts. While babies know basic feelings like joy and frustration, toddlers start feeling jealousy and preschoolers experience fear of separation.

It is at that time where emotions become a big part of their world that teaching children emotional intelligence becomes necessary.

The importance of EQ in children's lives

In theory, teaching emotional intelligence to children is great and all but what are the actual benefits of doing that?

A better grasp of emotions

At such a young age, children can get easily scared or confused by what they feel. Think about how toddlers start tearing up when they feel tired or how school age children feel abandoned when they get jealous when their best friend gets close to another child.

The idea is to teach them that their feelings are normal and valid and to teach them how to handle their emotions and cope with them and therefore, increasing their EQ.

When your child shows signs of distress over an emotion, take a moment to speak to them. Ask them why they think they feel the way they do and explain that it's alright for them to feel that way and that they shouldn't feel bad over it.

They handle others' emotions better

It is true that children are very sheltered at such an age, but though they aren't as perceptive as adults, they can be very smart. They are very aware of how we act and how their peers behave and they usually are quite sensitive. Did your child ever bring you their Teddy Bear to comfort you after a bad day at work? Beyond being a sweet gesture, that behavior is a sign of a promising EQ. When children learn to pay attention to others' emotions, they also learn to handle them better.

They can help and comfort others and learn from their peers' experiences.

They learn how to establish social relationships

It is very important to teach children how to behave with others to some extent as that would directly affect their ability to fit in and make friends. Thinking back to our childhood, the most popular children are the ones who always took the initiative to introduce themselves, were thoughtful enough to include others in their games and offer their help when others appeared to need it...

Likewise, it is important for children to respect authority figures such as their parents, teachers and the like and to obey those people. It is critical to learn at a young age that any disrespectful behavior is unacceptable and intolerable, not only because they are their elders but also because those people have some measure of control of their lives. It goes without saying, elders have more wisdom through experiences to better guide children in a direction which is beneficial for their overall well-being.

Show, don't tell

No matter how many times you instruct children on something, and regardless of how well you explain it, if you show them something other than what you preach, they will not listen so save yourself the trouble and teach them by doing it yourself.

It is a fact, at early childhood, kids learn by observing and imitating. We find it cute when a three-year-old grabs a newspaper and sits with legs crossed, a serious frown on their face but that proves that they like to act like the adults in their lives.

If you want your child to read, put down your phone and grab a book. If you want them to become emotionally intelligent, show them by displaying your own EQ.

Take them with you when you interact with other people. Show them what compassion is. Take them to a soup kitchen and teach them the value of helping those who are less fortunate. When you disagree with your spouse, show them how you can solve problems through communication and reason.

There will be times where the neighbors will come complaining to you about your child who hit their daughter, use that opportunity to explain to your child that behaviors like that are unacceptable and ask them if they would like to be on the receiving end. Then teach them how to acknowledge their mistakes and apologize.

Chapter 4. Dangers of Reduced Social Intelligence

It is a fact that your quality of life will suffer if you have a low EQ. Whether in the workplace or in your personal life, reduced social intelligence will make it more difficult for you to navigate the real world.

Coming across as unprofessional

While some people believe that they should be judged solely on their performance, it is simply not the case. If you are arrogant, rude and unkind, you will be labeled as unprofessional even if your work is flawless. Why? Because behaving in a way that doesn't take into account the emotions of those who you interact with may lead them to being uncomfortable dealing with you (and unless they have very thick skin, it is the most likely outcome). This also has a high probability to also affect their performance which can also cause a hindrance to their own work flow.

Not only that, but if you lose your temper in the workplace, the results are much the same.

This disregard of the people around you and lack of self-control will surely cause some issues as society tends to favor those who can "play nice" and possess a certain amount of professional courtesy in the workplace.

If you ever find yourself in a similar situation, sincerely apologize and make sure that your behavior doesn't repeat itself. There often is a low threshold or tolerance for disrespectful behavior, which inevitably will lead to termination of employment.

Offending Unintentionally

It can be very easy for people with mediocre social intelligence to say or do the wrong thing without even realizing it. It's difficult to take a hint when you can't read the mood. Most of the time, it is done without any malicious intent but what may seem like an innocent comment to you, may insult others. Often times, you can't afford to offend the people around you, especially in a professional context.

If you are told that what you said is offensive, apologize immediately. Even if you think you didn't do anything wrong, the fact is your behavior may have negatively affected someone and unfortunately you can't decide how other people feel. So, if you're told you were rude, don't make it worse trying to explain how you weren't rude, but instead focus on presenting a decent apology to make amends. This is a far better approach to quickly resolving an issue than letting it spiral out of control by turning into an endless argument.

Social isolation

They may not be aware of it, but some people have social skills that others deem lacking. We tend to label those people as "awkward", "weird" or even "creepy" and we usually avoid them. It may be unfair, but as humans, we tend to judge negatively that which we do not understand or feel is "out of the social norm". Now, some of those people may be fine with the social isolation and in that case, good for them! But some are also not content with missing out on socializing or not being included.

If you encounter someone like that, and are open to hearing some ways to become more social, then try helping them out by giving little hints on what they could do to improve their situation.

On the other hand, if you find yourself to be one of those people, then keep an open eye for anyone who might be trying to genuinely help you out in that way.

Sometimes, it is just a matter of being pushy or coming across as too eager and since people appreciate space and boundaries, maintaining a reasonable distance may solve your problem.

Actionable Tips!

Here are a few tips you can provide as suggestions (and of course you can use them too!):

1. **Ask Open-Ended Questions**

   One of the best ways to shift the conversation away from you and open the dialogue for further, simply ask open-ended questions. You'll find that if you ask a question that can be answered with a simple "Yes" or "No" the conversation doesn't go very far. Open ended questions encourage the other person to continue the conversation. A few examples of open-ended questions:

"What is your favorite memory from childhood?"
"What sights do you expect to see on your vacation?"
"How will you help the company if you are hired to work for us?"

2. Behave Like a Social Person

You can pretend to behave like a social person even if you don't feel like it. Make a conscious effort to talk to new people. Don't allow anxiety to keep you down. You'll be surprised how painless after getting it over with. Over time, it will become easier and easier and you'll quickly start improving your social skills.

3. Make Strides in Small Steps

Practice making small talk incrementally. Every small gesture and effort is a win. This may be as simple as thanking the cashier while checking out. You don't need to go to a huge event or party just to make progress.

4. People love talking about themselves, leverage it

It's a fact that most people *love* talking about themselves. It's a subject we know most about so simply asking someone about their family, career, hobbies or musical tastes can easily get the ball rolling. From there just show genuine interest about what they're saying. Continue asking questions about them while listening intently and you'll be well on your way to becoming an excellent conversationalist!

5. Offer Compliments Often and Many

A nice gesture or compliment can go a long way, not to mention an easy opportunity for further conversation. Offer a colleague an unexpected compliment on a task they completed or perhaps a presentation he or she did.

Sabotaging personal relationships

Some people in our lives accept us and love us unconditionally, this doesn't mean that our actions don't hurt them. People with low EQ are usually self-centered, they don't pay attention to those who are around them and that may translate as neglect. The people you love will try to find reasons for that neglect and they may start thinking that you are losing interest in having them in your life, that you don't care or that they are being too clingy; as a result, they may become distant.

Relationships are exchanges or two-way streets and you can't keep taking without giving back. And while you know you love the people in your life and you wish them no harm, you have to show them that you listen to them, care about them and are ready to pay attention to their emotional needs.

Actionable Tip!

When it comes down to it, life is about experiences and relationships. The relationships we have also shape our view on the world. These days we become distracted by everything and it's easy to let some of these relationships fall to the waist side by not staying in contact. An easy way to stay in contact or rekindle a relationship with someone you haven't spoken to in a while is to send them a very simple, yet thoughtful message:

> *"Hello _____, no response necessary. I just wanted to check in. I hope you're doing well. Let's catch up sometime soon. If there's anything you need or I can help you with, let me know. Otherwise, just saying hello."*

Chapter 5. Giving and receiving feedback

We often hear that communication is key when it comes to maintaining a good relationship. And it is true, feedback is necessary for progression to take place and no one will tell you otherwise. It is, however, important to know what to say and how to say it to encourage growth in social and professional settings.

What is feedback

Essentially, to give feedback to someone is to let them know what you think of their behavior or actions. It can be about how they conducted themselves or about a task they performed or anything that can be improved. In order for feedback to bear fruit, it should be delivered in a way that pushes towards improvement. You can often see that sort of feedback referred to as constructive criticism.

For example, when a teacher corrects a written expression, they are giving feedback to the student who wrote it. They correct any mistakes and write little notes and suggestions as well as words of motivation.

In a similar fashion, a supervisor may review the work employees they are overseeing and informs them of what to change, what to improve and lets them know, objectively, how they might be using the wrong approach.

Even in the household, when a parent corrects their child's behavior, they are giving them feedback. And when we think about it, educating a child is mostly teaching them and giving feedback on how should they apply what they have learned.

How to effectively deliver feedback

As we mentioned above, in order for feedback to produce the desirable results it must be worded properly. Good, uplifting feedback will often lead to a boost of motivation whether it is considered positive or negative feedback.

While positive feedback is relatively easy, giving negative feedback can be tricky. But it is the latter that is more consequential and must be attended to. Not to say that positive feedback is not important, of course.

As long as you speak objectively and you aim for progress, the person who is on the receiving end will take your words at face value and will probably listen and make the necessary changes. Remember that you can affect how well they take it through your manners, tone and expressions. The key to making the recipient more receptive to your suggestions is to speak calmly, confidently and appear comfortable while always beginning with positive things they are doing.

Delivering positive feedback

Let them know exactly what you appreciated and make sure it is something you want to see reflected again. This will help them keep in mind what you are looking for and what is considered desirable and a good practice.

Make sure you are being straightforward in your praise. You don't want to sound patronizing by exaggerating a person's accomplishments.

Deliver the feedback in private. Remember your school days? Very few of us liked being the teacher's pet! Even though you might believe that it is something to take pride in, they might not feel comfortable being the center of attention in a public venue and it is that much more valuable when done in private as they know you are being sincere and not putting up a show of being a good mentor.

Delivering negative feedback

As alluded to above, it is helpful to encase negative feedback within a positive one. The more optimal approach it to highlight what the person is doing correctly instead of delivering all negative observations in a row. This approach consequently, is a sure way for the conversation to go poorly. So, focus on the positive first to avoid taking a hit at someone's self-esteem. As a general rule of thumb, many would say that the last piece of criticism you deliver should always be positive. But, let's think about this for a second.

Actionable Tip!

If you're delivering a "feedback sandwich" which looks like:

1. Recipient gets a positive message
2. Recipient then gets negative feedback
3. Recipient then gets more positivity

This approach often causes the recipient to take negative feedback less seriously or with a grain of salt. We often remember the last thing we are told and if it's on a positive note, the negative feedback is mostly likely going to either fall on deaf ears or be forgotten shortly thereafter. This also leads to a false sense of progress.

Let's avoid this at all costs! Instead, focus on providing constructive feedback that resonates and sticks with the person. In fact, when constructive criticism is given properly, people are more appreciative because they understand that the criticism is coming from a place of good intentions and meant to help them become better.

Make sure you say what you have to say in a natural, non-threatening way. You don't want whomever you are speaking to think that mistakes will lead to harsh consequences. You want them to want to spot their mistakes and work to correct them and you want them to view feedback as a tool in their journey towards success and to seek it, ideally from different sources.

Wording your feedback thoughtfully doesn't mean you have to sugar coat your words, however. It is always best to be straightforward and specific. Do not give vague feedback that might make your subject feel lost; feedback is supposed to guide them in a precise way.

Try to offer a solution whenever you can. If you can't, let them know exactly what you think should be improved and they might already know how to go about it.

Make sure you are criticizing a behavior or an action and not a personality trait. It is about what they do, not who they are. Furthermore, criticizing them as a person would come across as you being personal about it and you don't want to seem petty like that.

Do not be rude. Besides potentially harming your interlocutor's performance and giving the impression that you are harassing them, speaking rudely will give a bad image of you first and foremost.

When giving criticism, sooner is always better than later. You don't want them to keep making that mistake and letting them know about it fast, will lead to a fast correction. Delaying that process will lead to embarrassment at best and important losses at worst.

Make sure you deliver the critiques in private. There is no point in doing it in public and they might be uncomfortable in that kind of setting and end up being too distracted to listen to what you have to tell them.

Receiving feedback

Know the importance of feedback. Make sure you understand that it is an important asset in the process of improvement. You don't want to be that person who stays stuck in one place because you couldn't stomach an honest suggestion designed to help you improve. The person giving you feedback is taking time out of their day to help you make progress, make sure you don't take that for granted and pay attention to what is being said to you.

Actionable Tip!

> Seek feedback. Sometimes, it's hard to get feedback depending on the setting. You might be self-employed and don't have a monthly assessment or work as a freelancer and your clients might not be experts in your field. It is up to you to make the effort of seeking feedback!

There are many ways you can put yourself in a position for feedback. Sometimes, from family and friends and if that's not an option, get creative! In this day and age, there are several means of communication that are available to everyone. This can be as simple as posting on social media or forums.

Be humble when receiving positive feedback. Yes, we know! It's great to hear words of praise and you start feeling invincible. Just remember to come back to earth once the feeling of euphoria wears off. Express your gratitude to the person who took the time to let you know that you're doing a good job and don't act cocky lest you make them regret their words, no one likes a show off.

Take criticism gracefully. It might be a hit to your ego, but deep down, you know that you are merely human and are as capable of making mistakes as the rest of us. Accept that you did something wrong and move on by correcting that behavior. Thank the person who let you know you were mistaken, you might not see it immediately, but they saved you a lot of embarrassment by letting you know about your mistakes early on.

Let them know that you are approachable. This is particularly important when you are in a leadership position. It's very easy to be intimidated by the boss, even when you think they are doing something wrong. Make sure the people around you know that you are willing to learn from them and can take criticism. Not only will they feel comfortable in an environment where their concerns are attended to, they will also seek you out in the future in case they need help or to solve a conflict, making it easier for you to do your job. After all, it wouldn't reflect well on you if you could dish it out but couldn't take it.

Conclusion

Emotional intelligence is the factor that will take you from being a smart person to a successful person. Having empathy and being able to work within a group and garner respect by paying attention to others' emotions and using them to your advantage will make for a better environment. Likewise, in your personal life, the ability to pay attention to your and people's emotions and respond to them properly will make you and everyone around you happier. We all say we want to see good people in the world. We want to be with those people, work with them and rely on them. It is time to change that way of thinking and become one of those people instead of hoping to meet them. Be the kind of person you want to share a relationship with. Be the kind of leader you needed when you started work. Be the best parent that you can to your children and be the best version of yourself. Be patient, reasonable, compassionate and all the good qualities that boost your Emotional Quotient.

Book 2.

Social Anxiety

A Guide to Social Anxiety: Easy and Effective Daily Strategies for Overcoming Social Anxiety and Shyness, Depression, Increase Happiness and Build Successful Relationships

INTRODUCTION

In this day and age, it is almost inevitable to get overwhelmed by the influx of new information that tell us how bad the world has become; look no further than your email, social media, television, newspapers, etc. Add that to the constant stress from work and personal life and having to deal with all sorts of problems and it is no surprise that you end up with mental disorders like depression and social anxiety.

The worst part is, we have gotten so used to living in these chaotic conditions that these disorders have become the norm in our lives, so much that we are unable to recognize them.

The reality is, it's not healthy to be in a constant state of misery and always on edge. It is highly important to be able to tell when we our loved ones are going through a difficult time. The ability to recognize someone who you love (or even you for that matter) has developed a condition will allow you to take the necessary steps to overcome said condition.

Social Anxiety Disorder is one of the most widespread mental disorders people deal with in recent times. It is an intense fear of being in social situations and though fear may help you perform better in some situations where its presence is reasonable and justified, the fear that socially anxious people experience is a response to events that are considered harmless and perfectly normal.

In some cases, situations such as making small talk with someone you recently met or introducing yourself to a potential business partner may seem highly dreadful, which can become a significant problem if it affects your social life negatively. Unfortunately, this often leads to making things more difficult than they should be.

Those who struggle to cope with social anxiety on a daily basis will often tell you they constantly overthink simple situations, over-analyze, and tend to think of the worst-case scenario.

Throughout time, human evolution has allowed us to develop a "fight or flight" response, or a physical response to a strong feeling of fear caused by a dangerous situation. Once upon a time, when humans needed to survive in the wild amongst dangerous creatures and surrounded by capricious natural conditions, this response allowed them to fight and defend themselves or run to escape from certain death. This response was characterized by a high heart rate, increased blood flow and hyperventilation, things that are supposed to make the anticipated physical exertion easier. However, when you experience the "fight or flight" response in a garden at a friend's wedding when you're introduced to one of their relatives, with no sign of any threat to your well-being, you can guess that something is wrong. You can imagine the scenario as your palms become sweaty and the words you know you want to say just can't seem to come out.

Once you have managed to identify and admit the fact that there is a problem, it becomes easier to look for a solution. No one out there will tell you that it is normal to be afraid of your newlywed's friendly 80-year-old grandmother as she tells you about her newest grandchild. Surely, she doesn't pose a threat, which leads you to ask yourself what is causing the problem. This means these feelings of fear and panic are coming from within. In other words, the perceived danger is only in your head. Although you may think this is counterintuitive, but in fact it is good news because you have the ability to completely control this situation. Once you address the problem and correct it, everything will naturally fall back into place. Your social life will prosper and the fear of dealing with people at work or in your personal life will be a thing of the past.

While Social Anxiety Disorder may vary from one person to another, it can progressively get worse and turn into something very serious. You may have heard about, witnessed, or even experienced it yourself: panic attacks. Also known as anxiety attacks, they are intense physical reactions to a stressful situation. While panic attacks are not exclusive to those who suffer from social anxiety, they are more frequently observed in that category. You hear of people freezing up when having to give a speech in front of a crowd, some sweat excessively, shake, stutter when speaking and even faint while trying to get through the event. You might think that you have a firm grasp of the situation and that it won't get that bad for you, but in most cases, things occur when we least expect them. The solution is to address your social anxiety head on and take measures to minimize the chances of future occurrences.

By taking this approach, it will not only help you with your anxiety, it will make you more capable of handling stressful situations and enable you to manage your physical and emotional response to them.

Each day you will find yourself stronger than the last, slowly building up your arsenal to help you remain calm and finally be in control.

Indeed, there will always be factors that are beyond your control, what is more important is for you to develop the mental strength to control your internal state of mind and ultimately your physical responses to these situations. This book aims to help you do just that by providing you an understanding of what exactly is causing your social anxiety, why you feel the way you do and how to manage the disorder so it doesn't prevent you from enjoying your life.

Living with social anxiety can be an ongoing challenge, which is why it's solely up to you to take massive action and shape the reality you so desire. This book will guide you through this endeavor and you will be back in charge of your own life in no time. If you are ready to live a life without fear, not having to worry about others' disapproval, the thought of feeling rejected or not fitting in, removing the false belief that you have nothing to talk about and want to soothe the unbearable pain of social anxiety for good, then keep reading because it's time to take action right now!

Chapter 1. The Truth About Social Anxiety

You might feel you're the only with a problem, however to many people's surprise social anxiety is quite common. And, actually, many people struggle with these fears. When deconstructing social anxiety, it's been discovered that the situations which trigger the symptoms of social anxiety disorder are not all the same.

For some people they experience anxiety in common social situations. For others, anxiety is linked to specific social situations, like performing in front of an audience, speaking to strangers and mingling at parties.

Common social anxiety triggers include:

- Performing on stage
- Meeting new people
- Public speaking
- Attending parties or other social gatherings
- Being watched while doing something
- Being teased or criticized
- Talking with authority figures
- Being called on in class
- Going on a date

- Being the center of attention
- Making small talk
- Speaking in a meeting
- Taking exams
- Eating or drinking in public
- Speaking with "important people"
- Making phone calls
- Using public restrooms

One of the most common misconceptions about people suffering from social anxiety disorder is that they are shy. While it is easy to make that mistake when you are not close to that person, it is important to know the difference between social anxiety and shyness in order to recognize it in yourself and in others.

Shyness Vs. Social Anxiety

What is shyness:

Shyness is a feeling of apprehension, unease or awkwardness around new people or in unfamiliar situations. It can be a result of self-esteem issues, sheltered upbringing or a fear of rejection. A shy person is often withdrawn and quiet in a new setting.

While shyness is inconvenient at first, it is often overcome after some time. Once you get a feel of your surroundings and the people you are associating with you become more comfortable and it gets easier to act as your true self.

As children, we were often shy when visiting strangers or in unfamiliar environments, hiding behind our parents and avoiding eye contact. However, when the people we visit would speak to us kindly, invite us to play or draw us out with treats, we start to trust them, our guard is lowered and we become more comfortable talking to them. Ironically, in the end, we are usually reluctant to leave our new friends.

What is social anxiety?

The fact that it is also known as social phobia tells you all you need to know about this disorder.

Did You Know?

Social anxiety disorder, also known as social phobia, is currently the third largest psychological problem in the United States. Millions of people quietly endure this pain every single day, believing there is no hope of them getting better.

It is a very common mental disorder, often described as an overwhelming fear of being judged. The disorder also encompasses the fear of being embarrassed and humiliated in social situations, being the center of attention, or offending people around them.

For example, if you are terrified of starting a conversation, what you might really fear is saying something that would offend the other party or even worse something embarrassing that may lead them to judge you.

Sometimes, that fear manifests itself through physical symptoms like sweating, shaking and dizziness. This can make your life particularly difficult as it can get so intense that you might not be unable to function properly.

A socially anxious person finds social situations very straining and they either circumvent that strain by avoiding socializing altogether or try to handle it at the expense of their mental health as they tend to overthink a lot.

Overthinking can occur before, during and after a social interaction. Typically, what tends to happen is that you keep thinking of different scenarios before the interaction. During the conversation you self-consciously think about whether you are doing alright and think of what you should have done differently after. This behavior is very unhealthy as it can distract you from important tasks and shackle your freedom of enjoying life.

Is it shyness or social anxiety?

It is true that the two have many characteristics in common and while both are the cause of a lot of discomfort, it is necessary to know the difference in order to know how to handle the two conditions.

Social anxiety is often written off as shyness which prevents it from being diagnosed and managed adequately. 75% of people who suffer from social anxiety disorder do not receive treatment mainly because they don't realize they suffer from the disorder in the first place.

To try and find out whether you suffer from social anxiety or mere shyness, ask yourself the following questions:

1. **How afraid are you?**

   If you feel nervous right before or during a social situation but can keep it together, you might suffer from shyness. Try to pay attention to whether or not the feeling subsides after a while and see if you feel more at ease speaking with the people you are with. If the nervousness persists and is accompanied by other symptoms like shaking, erratic heartbeat, sweating and an inability to speak eloquently, it might be more serious and you might have social anxiety.

2. **Is there a timeframe in which you feel anxious?**

   Another helpful pointer is the time frame. If you experience nervousness right before getting involved in a social situation, it is most likely shyness. People who suffer from social anxiety tend to feel that fright days, weeks and even months beforehand. Constant worry and loss of sleep are frequently experienced through that time.

3. **How much do you avoid people?**

   A shy person might not directly seek strangers or might be unable to start a conversation but they often wish to make new acquaintances and be included in social activities. The fact that they don't initiate contact is caused by a lack of confidence and not because they don't want to get involved in social situations.

A socially anxious person on the other hand might actively avoid socializing. However, it is not because they refuse to get to know a new person in itself, rather it is due to the intense fear of going about it the wrong way and saying something offensive or embarrassing.

Additionally, overthinking can also take its toll on them and avoiding social settings is a way of protecting themselves from it.

If you the prospect of going somewhere new and meeting new people makes you a bit nervous, it is probably just shyness. If you go as far as making excuses to avoid being in a social setting, it is social anxiety.

4. How is it affecting your life?

A shy person might come across as awkward, weird or even arrogant at the beginning however, that first impression is often overridden when you get to know them. Have you ever heard anything along the lines of "I thought you were rude when I first met you?" That is usually a good indication that shyness took over and you we're at your best moment. The fact that you've been told this means you managed to turn the situation in your favor after you got more comfortable speaking to them.

Socially anxious people often do not have that luxury. They tend to avoid people, not making any new friendships and distancing themselves from anyone attempting to get to know them. This situation can escalate very quickly for the worse in which simple and brief social interactions such as ordering a drink at the local coffee shop becomes daunting.

While "shy" is often used as an adjective to describe someone, often by the person in question, anxiety is a mental disorder. Shy people often accept shyness as a part of their character but people suffering from social anxiety are too negatively affected by the disorder to embrace it as readily.

From shyness to social anxiety

It's been discovered that roughly 50% of those who suffer from social anxiety say they are shy. Keep in mind that it is also possible for acute shyness to develop into social anxiety.

Shyness tends to exhibit the following characteristics

- Blushing
- Acting quiet
- Looking away
- Awkward laugh
- Fidgeting.

Shyness is innate or encouraged in the upbringing. While on the other hand anxiety is triggered by some type of event. In other words, social anxiety has a starting point.

Physical signs and symptoms of Social Anxiety:

- Trembling or shaking (including shaky voice)
- Red face, or blushing
- Heart racing or tightness in chest
- Sweating or hot flashes
- Shortness of breath
- Faint or feeling dizzy
- Upset stomach, nausea, "butterflies in your stomach"

Getting the jitters is completely normal before giving a speech. However, if you have social anxiety the determining factor might be that you worry for weeks in advance, start immensely shaking during a speech that you can hardly speak or even call in sick to get out of it.

Emotional signs and symptoms of social anxiety disorder

- Excessive self-consciousness and anxiety in everyday social situations
- Before an upcoming social situation experiencing intense worry for days, weeks, or even months ahead of time
- Extreme fear of being judged or watched by others (Especially by people you don't know)

- Fear that you will act in ways that would embarrass or humiliate yourself
- Fear that others will notice that you're nervous

Behavioral signs and symptoms:

- Drinking before social situations in order to soothe your nerves
- Avoiding social situations so much that it disrupts your life or limits your activities
- Keeping quiet or hiding in the background in order to escape notice and embarrassment
- A need to always bring a friend along with you wherever you go

Chapter 2: Facing Social Anxiety

Let's dive further into social anxiety and the science behind it. Surprisingly, to outsiders what may seem to be a normal interaction, making small talk with the clerk at the grocery store, calling a business to get more information, can be a struggle for those suffering from social anxiety. Very few people actually understand the agonizing and torturous depth of social anxiety. However, these situations are not what one would classify as life and death, so why is social fear so bad?

Let's peel back the layers of the proverbial onion to better understand social anxiety.

If you have ever broken a bone, you may remember the occurrence, but the pain itself can be a challenge to remember and to relive. On the other hand, it's very easy to recall the last time you felt horrified in public. Well, there's a reason for this! Mental pain trumps physical pain. Rather, social pain is actually worse than physical pain simply because that experience continues to play over and over in your mind like a broken record. Think about it... Which would be more detrimental to your long-term health, breaking your bone once or having to relive a traumatic experience every day, several times a day?

Did You Know?

Individuals can reexperience social pain much more intensely and more easily than physical pain. Studies have shown people reported higher levels of pain after reliving a past socially painful event than after reliving a past physically painful event.

This remains true as just the thought of enduring a painful event is much more terrifying than the actual experience itself. Studies have also indicated that perceived job insecurity tallies as one of the most critical factors in employees' well-being and can even be more harmful than actually losing your job with subsequent unemployment.

You see it all comes down to an almond-shape set of neurons located deep in the brain's medial temporal lobe called the amygdala.

The amygdala has been shown to play an instrumental role in the processing of emotions and is linked to both fear responses and pleasure.

Anxiety, depression, autism, phobias and even post-traumatic stress disorder are all conditions suspected of being linked to abnormal functioning of the amygdala.

The typical advice given to combat social anxiety and fear by most sources is completely incorrect. Their advice?

Suppression.

Unfortunately, all this leads to is a decrease in your ability to experience positive feelings and augments negative feelings, in turn skyrocketing stress.

Which is why taking a different approach may just be the key.

There are a number of things you can do to actively counter social anxiety. Some of the following tips may work better than others, depending on what you are comfortable with. Use this list simply to inspire you to try different approaches and techniques that work best for you.

1. **Seeking help**

   Though Social Anxiety Disorder is one of the most common conditions out there, it is also one of the most tenacious. Seeking help from a professional can save you a lot of time and effort. Keep in mind that trained professionals have studied various mental conditions and have a solid understanding of how to deal with them efficiently. And, there is nothing wrong with asking for help (This cannot be stressed enough!). A therapist can help you unveil which approach and strategy has the highest likelihood of working for you.

2. **Identify the cause**

   While there is a possibility the condition developed overtime with a slow buildup of many stressful situations, your social anxiety could have also been triggered by just a traumatic singular event in your life. Even though it was not fully evident at the time, the impact may have been hard enough to cause this kind of damage.

   <u>Actionable Tip!</u>

   Close your eyes; try to think back and remember what happened in your past that could have possibly been the event which triggered everything. What made you feel that socializing is stressful? What harmed your self-esteem? What was the triggering event? Maybe you were supposed to sing a solo part with your class in primary school and forgot the words. Or perhaps you missed an easy shot when playing basketball that cost your team an important win. Looking back, it could have been something others would probably view as something that wasn't that big of a deal, but because you gave it so much importance it forever shaped your perception of reality as you know it. The point of this is once you can successfully pinpoint what the triggering event is you have the power to make change.

3. **Self-help manuals**

Additional books and self-help manuals can be a good medium to acquire the help you need. Knowledge is power. They provide a quick and actionable way to learn how to manage a situation before or as it arises. Ideally, those written by an expert in the field such as a psychiatrist or even a psychology professor is a good place to begin supplementing your learning.

Actionable Tip!

Often times these books have steps you can implement right away. The secret is to:

1. Read and fully understand the step
2. Take action and implement right away

With this approach it's a surefire way to see results quickly!

4. **Keep a journal**

Journal writing will provide you a way to track your thoughts and your progress. Hands down, there is no better way to learn about your thought processes than to keep a running record of them on paper. It can also be a helpful tool when it comes to identifying your triggers and avoiding them. If you are seeing a therapist, the journal will help the two of you make progress by being able to identify common patterns, emotions and potential triggers.

Actionable Tip!

Keeping track of your emotions doesn't have to be fancy, the point is to be able to track how you feel on a daily basis.

1. First draw two evenly spaced lines down the page from top to bottom and about an inch from the top draw a line across. This will create three even columns.
2. Label the first column "Situation / Event" at the top
3. Label the second column "Thoughts / What Story Am I Telling Myself?"
4. Label the third column "How anxious am I feeling?"

Now that you have the page setup, begin by dating each entry to accurately keep track of your progress. Now, anytime you begin to have a thought or get into a situation that makes you feel anxious, make sure to write it down! If you find it more helpful, you can even give your anxiety level a number on a scale of 1 to 10 instead.

Yes, it's quite impossible to write down *every* single emotion and thought you may have, however the more manageable approach is to take note of when you're feeling physical symptoms, such as sweaty palms perhaps the forehead, dizzy or even moderately anxious.

5. Do not seclude yourself

At first staying at home and shielding yourself from any possible interaction and the real world may seem like an excellent idea, but in fact it's not. There's a reason that correctional facilities and prisons use solitary confinement because it is deemed as one of the most painful punishments.

It is very easy to fall into the bad habit of staying at home with a nice book and your preferred beverage, avoiding any sort of interaction with all human beings. Progress is about pushing the envelope and leaving your comfort zone. In fact, it has been found that this uncomfortable zone often times is where one gets the best results for their efforts. So, if you want to do something about your social anxiety, staying at home and avoiding social situations is a step in the wrong direction.

6. Take initiative

Yes, it's difficult. But so are many other things in life. Give yourself the little push to find social situations that you can barely even think about. Greet one of the vendors on your way to work. Offer help to your colleague who is struggling with a stack of folders. Introduce yourself to the new head of your division. Remember the thought is worse than the actual action. You will be surprised how a little initiative will go a long way.

7. Be prepared

Having a plan gives you a way to not only track your progress, but to set goals for yourself as well. Chances are, not everything will go according to plan being that there will be variables you cannot control, people, for example.

Actionable Tip!

I'm sure at some point you have felt concerned about what to talk about in a social situation in the fear that you may not have anything to say at all! This is where having a plan and a few general questions in your arsenal will not only break the ice, but can ensure to keep the conversation moving along smoothly.

Here are a few easy topics to get you started:

1. I've been looking for a beautiful dress just like that. Where did you get it?
2. I've been going to the same place for lunch forever. Do you have any recommendations?
3. Do you know of a cool coffee shop nearby?
4. How do you _______ at this party?

5. I want to see a movie this weekend. Have you seen anything good lately?
6. I've been wanting to read that book! Are you familiar with the author?
7. I'm not sure which drink to order. How do you like what you're drinking?
8. Oh, my goodness! Your dog is adorable.
9. Which bands are you here to see?
10. I love your shoes!
11. We need another person to join our trivia team! Would you be interested?
12. I'm going to play some music on the jukebox. What song should I play?
13. I love this instructor! Have you taken any of her other classes?
14. Do you know how to get to Market Street? I'm a bit lost.
15. Can I get your thoughts on this gift?
16. I saw you when I walked in and I just wanted to come over and say hello.

Although not required, it certainly helps to talk about popular topics such as current news or sports. Keeping the conversation about subjects your conversational partner is interested in makes for a smooth and effortless interaction. If you can't seem to find a topic they're interested in, simply ask them what they do for fun! As mentioned earlier, people *love* talking about themselves. Be inquisitive and genuinely interested about them, their family or any of their other interests.

8. Bring your Wing person

A wing man or woman can also serve as an asset and a great way to give you an extra boost of confidence. It doesn't even have to be a friend in common, someone who is good at social settings will be a great help too and will smooth things out in social settings. They will literally stand by your side and support you in many situations such as a meeting, networking event, conference, a birthday party, wedding, or while out at a bar on a Saturday night.

A good wingman will approach people for you and break the ice. You can follow their lead and chime in on the conversation. This helps you to make meaningful connections and build relationships that truly matter.

<u>The Importance of a Wingman</u>

A. Networking: They can be advantageous to your career. A wingman can position you to meet valuable people who will want to connect and support your success. It's also like having a second pair of eyes to be on the lookout for potential job opportunities or ways to help you advance professionally.

B. **Accountability**: Breaking through your social anxiety is that much easier when you have someone to keep you accountable for your actions and the goals you as a team have set out to achieve.

C. **Credibility**: A wingman can give you credibility just by association and their own social proof. This is truly invaluable for those introductions to the people who may seem "untouchable" or frighten you to approach on your own. If your confident wingman has executed correctly, the person you're being introduced to will feel like they're the one getting the most benefit from it! This is a very powerful technique and can ease the social anxiety almost instantly.

D. **Mentorship**: Someone who has more experience than you who provides advice can shorten your learning curve to a fraction of the time. Instead of trying to figure out how to beat your social anxiety by yourself or fumble through numerous conversations, let a mentor guide you.

E. **Confidence**: Going to an event with a wingman will drastically change your self-confidence. Not only because you have a companion, but they're also with you to make you look great. It's like the advice from Will Rogers: "Get someone else to blow your horn and the sound will carry twice as far."

F. Freedom: Even after taking the plunge to introduce yourself, you may find that an interaction with someone is not going as well as you had hoped. This is where the wingman can swoop in and rescue you! Releasing you from the imaginary shackles that bind you to an uncomfortable conversation or situation can easily be done with the help of your trusty wingman. It may be a good idea to come up with a cue or signal you can communicate with your wingman to initiate this process. Some examples could be blinking a few times, snapping your fingers once, a secret word or even a simple cough.

9. Practice confidence

Fake it until you make it! Those words didn't become popular for nothing. Make eye contact, have good posture and speak with a clear and understandable voice. With this technique you are rewiring your brain to actually believe you are confident. Research has shown that your thoughts and what you believe are very powerful. Before you know it, you won't even have to pretend anymore! Confidence comes from within, just keep in mind that you are a smart, talented and kind person who has the ability to achieve anything and is worthy of respect and attention.

10. Test your limits

Put your learnings in to action! Simply reading or watching videos about how to overcome social anxiety is worthless if you don't put it into practice. You can read all the self-help books in the world but your progress will remain the same if you don't immediately apply. Progress is often made outside of your comfort zone. Pushing yourself to expand your horizons and get a little better each day is critical to growth.

It's often easier to take small steps to break outside of our comfort zone with a mentor or support team. As mentioned above, you know how important a mentor can be to your overall break through. If you know someone who can encourage and help you along the way, they can make these changes seem less daunting.

Progress does not have to happen in strides which is why you should experiment a little bit at a time. The breakthrough and healing process may require you to endure several uncomfortable experiences, but that is a key component to your success.

CHAPTER 3: PRACTICAL EXERCISES TO COMBAT SOCIAL ANXIETY

While it may appear as if there's nothing you can really do about the symptoms of social anxiety disorder or social phobia, quite actually, there are several things that can help or at least limit its effect on your life. The first step is challenging your mentality.

Sufferers of social anxiety have negative thoughts and beliefs that add fuel to their fears and anxiety. Some examples of these thoughts are:

- "I know I'm going to wind up looking like a fool."
- "My voice will start shaking and I'll embarrass myself."
- "People will think I'm an idiot"
- "I'll seem boring because I won't have anything to say."

Deliberately confronting these negative thoughts is a powerful way to reduce the symptoms of social anxiety.

Actionable Tip!

Step 1: Pinpoint the underlying negative thoughts of your fear and social situations. If you're stressed about an upcoming presentation, the underlying negative thought may be: "I'm going to screw it all up. Everyone is going to think I'm completely worthless."

Step 2: Confront and dissect these thoughts. Make an effort to ask yourself questions about these negative thoughts.

- "Do I know with complete certainty I'm going to ruin the presentation?"
- "Just because I'm nervous, does that mean people will believe I'm inadequate?"

Exploring your negative thoughts using logical evaluations will allow you to slowly replace them with positive and more realistic ways of looking at social situations that trigger your anxiety.

The better we understand why we feel and think a certain way and how that ultimately acts as triggers will help mitigate their negative impact on your life.

Negative thinking styles that fuel social anxiety

Below are a few thought patterns which tend to worsen social anxiety. It is imperative that you avoid falling victim to the following unhelpful thinking styles:

- **Personalizing** – The assumption people are negatively focusing on you or having the belief that whatever is happening with other people has something to do with you.

- **Fortune telling** – Trying to predict the future, often while assuming the worst will happen. You're already anxious beforehand because you can just "feel" the situation is going to turn out terribly.

- **Mind reading** – The belief that you know what other people are thinking. Leading you to think they see you in the same negative way you see yourself.

- **Catastrophizing** – Exaggerating the severity of issues or making a big deal out of nothing.

Be aware of your surroundings and the people you are with:

Paying attention to the person you are talking with will allow you to focus on the moment and it will keep the negative thoughts you have about yourself at bay. This will also allow you to live in the moment instead of overthinking about the impression you're giving off. It also directs your thoughts to what they are saying and how to help or encourage them. Paying such genuine attention to your partner will also make them feel valued and that's a plus.

Speak to those who you trust:

While talking to a licensed therapist is certainly ideal, you can also talk to a friend or a loved one if getting professional help is not an option. It helps you unburden yourself at your own pace and you can share as much or as little as you are comfortable with. Sometimes, having the ability to speak the words out loud to someone else without judgement to get rid of the frustration can help you break the cycle of anxious thoughts you have to deal with when you are on your own. An outsider has an objective view of what troubles you and sometimes, hearing how insignificant a problem is from someone else is more convincing than telling yourself the same thing.

Be positive:

You hear it all the time, stay positive. Focusing on your strengths and good points will not only keep you in a positive mindset, it will boost your confidence and self-esteem. If you focus your thinking on positivity, you won't have time to think about what is bad.

Actionable Tip!

As a conscious exercise think about and write down five things that you are grateful for, like and appreciate about yourself. These can even be some accomplishments. Try to increase the number of these qualities every day. After some time, being positive will become a habit.

Don't take yourself too seriously:

This doesn't mean that you shouldn't be serious, far from it. Rather, try not to take your mistakes too seriously, take it easy and don't be too harsh on yourself. If you mispronounce something for instance, laugh it off and move on. People will take it as seriously as you do and your reaction about a mishap usually shapes theirs. So, lighten up!

Big brother is the only one who's watching you:

Your anxiety makes you think that everyone is watching you, waiting for you to commit some major sin but the truth is, everyone is too busy worrying about themselves to track your every move. No one saw you trip on the sidewalk and no, those two guys who are walking behind you are not laughing about you.

However, what if they were?

Certainly, this is easier said than done, right? Let's assume for argument's sake that people are watching you. (Which is definitely not the case by the way). So, people are watching you and judging your every move, right? So, what? Why does that matter? How are they relevant? Why does their opinion matter? The simple answer is that it doesn't. Those people do not matter. They aren't close to you in anyway. They are just some stranger that you happened to share a space with for a very short time. Let them judge you if they dare, it won't affect you in any way, shape or form.

Be nice to yourself:

Often times, our brain likes to play mental games with us for some reason. It's up to you to fight that and to be good to yourself. Treat yourself as you would treat a very dear friend. Treat yourself, praise yourself, give yourself pep talks and cheer yourself up.

Relax:

It is very important to interrupt any physical symptoms of anxiety before they turn into something worse. When you start experiencing that feeling of panic, take a moment to regulate your breathing and to calm down. Relax. Try to add meditation to your daily routine as it will be very beneficial and help you keep the stress at bay.

Keep in mind that anxiety actually isn't as visible as you may think. Even if someone notices that you're nervous, that does not mean they will think poorly of you. Chances are other people are feeling just as nervous as you or for that matter have felt the same way in the past.

Control Your Breathing

There are many changes that happen in your body when you become anxious. One of the first noticeable changes is you begin to breathe quickly. Hyperventilation or over breathing will throw off the balance of oxygen and carbon dioxide in your body. This leads to more physical symptoms of anxiety, such as a feeling of suffocation, increased heart rate, dizziness, and muscle tension.

Actionable Tip!

Slowing your breathing down will help bring your physical symptoms of anxiety back under control.

Use the following breathing exercise to help you remain calm:

1. With your back upright and your shoulders relaxed sit comfortably.

2. Place one hand on your chest and the other in the middle of your stomach.

3. While filling your lungs to capacity, slowly inhale through your nose for 5 seconds. The hand on your stomach should rise, while the hand on your chest should not move very much.

4. Hold your breath for 3 seconds.

5. Slowly exhale through your mouth for 6 seconds, pushing out as much air as possible. Your hand on your stomach should move in as you exhale, while your other hand should move very little.

6. Continue to breathe in through your nose and out through your mouth. Maintain focus keeping a slow and steady breathing pattern of 5 seconds in, 3 seconds holding, and 6

seconds out.

Conclusion

Thank you for reading this book. Your journey to self-improvement has only begun. Hopefully, this was an educational read and taught you more about social anxiety.

Life will always throw some unexpected curveballs in your direction and it is up to you how you deal with them.

Now that you have a better understanding of Social Anxiety Disorder, it's time for you to put the tips and pointers you picked up from this book into action. Practice makes perfect as they say, so go out and mingle. Take it easy at first, even 10 minutes a day can make a difference. Take a friend to help ease the mood and talk about a subject you are familiar with, whatever suits your fancy as long as you just take action. An object in motion stays in motion, therefore all you need to do is take the first step! Remember you are strong, powerful and courageous. Now get out there and become the person you know you can be.

Book 3.

Dating for Introverts

How to Become More Charismatic, Boost Your Confidence, Eliminate Dating Fear, Anxiety and Shyness with Simple Techniques

INTRODUCTION

Dating, you keep saying to yourself, is plagued with unnecessary anxiety and fraught with rejection. Not to mention how overwhelming the decisions can be. Where do you even start? Online dating, meetups, blind dates, the bar? Wait, definitely not the bar, that's far too intimidating.

Have you ever wondered how some people seem to get date after date after date while you can't seem to muster up the courage to even introduce yourself? How do you even get out of this situation?

There are plenty of books and resources with ambiguous information out there that claim to provide the "secret" to finding the person of your dreams.

There is a big problem with the common advice often given during conversations surrounding dating ... "Say yes to everything! Just get out there! Let everyone know you're looking for a significant other."

Although that cookie cutter advice is meant to be well-intentioned, it highly contradicts a major essential factor to an introvert's well-being — alone time.

As an introvert finding a significant other comes down to doing the exact opposite of what you love most – binge watching another Netflix murder mystery series in your favorite sweatpants. Now, the reality is if you really want a partner-in-crime, it means taking a leap of faith and mingling.

I get it, dating can be scary, and you'd rather be back at home than out in the real-world having conversations that you feel may end up going nowhere. A minefield of endless chit chat and pointless small talk. Because introverts don't thrive off and get the same boost of energy from social interactions as extroverts do, these conversations tend to feel like a waste of time.

This book will serve as a guide to help you navigate through the world of dating and make it a little less intimidating. By following the advice outlined in the following pages, you will be able to take what you previously thought were your weaknesses as an introvert and harness them to become your most powerful weapon to getting the date of your dreams.

CHAPTER 1. DRESS FOR SUCCESS

We are only as confident as we view ourselves. This statement cannot be stressed enough. If we don't view ourselves as confident, it will immediately be apparent in the way we dress, carry ourselves, use of facial expressions and even in the tone of our voice.

A man who clearly has difficulty dressing well with an average body composition can still charm his way through a conversation and leaving with the most stunning woman in the room. The power is in charisma and confidence. Do not take this lightly.

The good news is that charm and confidence are acquired through experience.

Understand those who you see having significant success were not born with these characteristics, in fact, quite the contrary. With a little practice you too can grow to learn how to effectively use these powerful tools and change your life forever.

So, let's get right to it.

The first step of this critical process is to improve the way you appear to other people. Your appearance is critical.

In all honesty, we can't all look like Tom Cruise or Jessica Alba, or have endless amounts of funds to get costly cosmetic surgery (Which is not recommended by the way). On the other hand, even if you did have enough money to pursue that route, it makes no sense if you're not confident in your own skin or lack charm. A better path would be to increase your physical fitness levels from nonexistent to a few days per week. With that said, you really don't even need to hit the gym to become confident in your ability to speak eloquently to others.

The more practical and fastest approach is to become more aware of how you dress yourself. The fact is that clothes play a major role in your presentation. If you're dressed well, many women will notice. On the other hand, if you're dressed poorly, they will inevitably notice that, too. This is a risk you take that may turn them off.

Think about it, our appearance gives people an idea of who we are. The first time you meet someone, their first impression and appearance are the only thing you have to base an opinion on them. The best part about this first impression is that you have the power to control those interactions.

You would be surprised at how much of a transformation you can make by simply adding a few carefully selected pieces of clothing to your wardrobe. All this takes is a small investment and a bit of guidance. The goal is to mesh your personality with a sense of style that radiates to the world who you are.

It is very important to dress for who you are. I have to admit that I am not the most stylish or most well-dressed out of my friends, but am comfortable in a style that makes me feel confident in who I am as a person. Wear what will make you feel great and boost your confidence while out in social environments.

Tips for clothes:

1. **Select colors that compliment your skin tone**

   Skin tone is the natural color of your skin. The color can change depending on the season, such as winter or the summer. You should always dress to be the best version of yourself.

2. **Get clothes that fit well and conform to your body type**

   This will help solve roughly 95% of your style problems. To be honest you could even get away with jeans and t-shirt as long as they conform to your body type. Better fitting clothes simply look better.

3. **Avoid anything that gives you anxiety or patterns that are overwhelming**

   Matching colors can go a long way. Too much pattern conflict can clash and make you look like you're in a circus act. Don't get me wrong, I love the circus and the performers are incredibly talented. However, that doesn't mean I'm looking to date a clown either.

4. **Dress to impress yourself. Looking in the mirror, you want to tell yourself, "Dang! I look GOOD!"**

   It all starts from the way you view yourself. If you tell yourself you look good, you will shine bright with positive energy and confidence.

5. **Press / iron your clothes**

   This is a no brainer, but too many people overlook or just don't care what they put on. Wrinkles in clothes is sloppy, makes you appear careless and cheap. Take the four or five minutes to press your clothes because it shows you care.

The point is that you want to dress to impress without losing who you are as a person. You may say to yourself, you're just not naturally stylish. But, surprise, no one is! It takes some experimenting.

In fact, most girls wish guys would just put a little effort into their appearance. Most guys dress so poorly that even that small bit of effort helps them stand out from the rest of the crowd. However, it is important to mention that dressing comfortably does not mean looking like a homeless person. You do not need to be dressed fancy as if you were to be walking down the line in a fashion show. Simply pay more attention to the way you dress, because others around you consciously and subconsciously will notice.

Be aware of your environment

Although this may be obvious, showing up to a casual event will call for a much different dress attire as opposed to a business networking event. You wouldn't wear sandals and a crop top to a business event, (unless it was a themed event where it was expected) because you would stand out in the worst kind of way. Make sense? You should always know what clothes are appropriate for the event you are attending. In case you are unaware, inquire for further information.

As mentioned previously, dress welling is a sure-fire way to boost your confidence and also creates a good impression of you while meeting new people.

Outside of special occasions and events, keeping your dress attire casual and comfortable is completely fine.

Chapter 2. The Power of Mindset

It is important to feel comfortable in your own skin first and foremost. Having a strong mindset and framing the world you live in can better prepare you to face the world head on with unshakeable confidence.

Every day the goal should be to become the best version of yourself. The ultimate goal is to live a life where you and the best version of yourself are not strangers, but constantly pushing and keeping up with each other.

With that said, the correct mindset is so important entire book series are dedicated to the subject alone. We are what we think and we only achieve what our limiting beliefs allow us to achieve. Mindset reinforces your ability to communicate clearly, know what you want and allows for enough space for you and others around you to become who you want to be.

When it comes down to it, dating is all about the number of people you meet. The more people you meet, the better idea you have of what it is you do and do not want in a partner. Although it has a negative connotation, dating is in fact a numbers game. If you only meet one person the likelihood of that person being the “one” is slim to none. Now, there is a chance the stars align in your favor and you meet the person of your dreams on the first attempt, but for the rest of us it’s not realistic.

Adjust Your Mindset

With a few simple shifts in how you approach dating can make a world of a difference. This can make things easier on both of you and allow for a more enjoyable experience.

1. **No more negative thoughts**

   Avoid telling yourself the same narrative over and over that you're terrible at dating. We all are terrible at first, it's just a fact of life. These negative thoughts set you up for failure right from the beginning. Instead, having positive thoughts about how much you will enjoy meeting new people and learning from their different perspectives on life.

   You don't have to go into the date hoping this person is the "one", but rather someone you could see being friends with first. The reality is that both of you are looking to find a partner, someone you could enjoy spending time doing activities and fun things together.

   As Norman Vincent, the author of the book, The Power of Positive Thinking, said "Change your thoughts and you change your world."

2. **Gratitude**

   Once you start loving who you are as a person and express gratitude for the things you *do* have, the faster you will be able to have meaningful and real relationships with others. Instead of placing all of your energy and attention on the things you don't have, focus on loving yourself and being thankful for all of the beautiful things in your life currently. You can start small by being thankful for the roof over your head, your friends and family, all the small wins in your daily life.

Gratitude should even stem from those who you have dated in the past, because without their influence on your life you wouldn't be who you are today. You wouldn't have had the opportunity to grow as a person and learn what you don't want in a partner, and contrarily what you ultimately *do* seek in a partner. Gratitude will also allow you to raise your inner vibrations, foster inner peace, forgive, forget and release resentment and anger.

3. **Use a dating journal**

   The dating journey is never a straight path and along the way will be a series of ups, downs, stopping and starting, you should be mindful of your experiences and document them to not only see progression, but to appreciate the lessons each one provides. Instead of seeing each experience as a failure, you will start to understand that you are on a purposeful journey.

   At the core, your success stems from your own growth and evolution during along this journey. Below are three questions to note in your journal after each date:

   - What did I enjoy about this date?
   - How did I learn more about myself from this person?
   - Did I learn anything from this person?

Use these entries as building blocks to form the foundation. When you actively seek what is beautiful in another person, being genuinely curious and reflect those learnings upon yourself, you will discover not only to love yourself more, but also will find love and compassion in unexpected places.

Start journaling your experiences! You'll thank me later.

4. **Switch up your routine**

Sometimes on my daily run, I will literally go out of my way to get lost. This forces me to break out of the mindless routine and experience something new. I find this keeps my mind active and a great way to switch things up. So, how does this relate to dating?

Let me ask you, when was the last time you switched up your routine and met someone or had an unexpected experience because you didn't follow your robot-like ways?

Switching it up can be a small as taking a different route to your job, running down a different street, going on an unexpected adventure, or even wearing a different color which may strike up a beautiful conversation.

This can go as far as expanding your network of friends by volunteering at a cause you feel is worthy of your time. Being a little more serendipitous can be invigorating, give you a boost of energy and confidence and better shape you for more social interactions. These different experiences can also be used as talking points making you a more interesting person!

The point is that as humans we tend to become comfortable in a routine that is monotonous and we often forget to spice things up. Do something different!

5. **Keep an open mind**

Drop the preconceived notions of what your "type" is and keep an open mind. When you let your guard down and open your heart the magic will start to happen. You see, the more filters and picky you are, the less likely you are to find a great match.

"I'm only attracted to brunettes.", "I have to marry someone of the same religious faith.", "I only date tall men."

Sounds familiar?

When it comes to dating, we preemptively make judgements about who we want to be with or avoid. The problem with this is that this kind of thinking can be self-sabotaging. If you put large constraints on your dating pool, you hinder your chances of finding happiness. Think about it, dating, in its most basic form, is about experimenting and testing things out. So, open up your heart and your mind and embrace different dating "types".

It's often the relationships in which the partners have the most differences that tend to be the happiest. So, get out there, drop the judgement and surprise yourself with a new dating type.

CHAPTER 3. STEPPING OUT INTO THE REAL WORLD

Dating forces an introvert to do the exact opposite of what you are comfortable doing, being social and interacting with other humans. No doubt this can be an overwhelming task to say the least. Which is why it is important to address the previous steps first.

You're armored with an unshakeable mindset and not only feeling comfortable in your new dress attire, but more importantly, in your own skin.

With this new boost of confidence, it's time to step out into the real world. Let's take it to the next level.

As you venture out into the social world, take notice of your environment and select your scene carefully. The night club may not be the best place to begin your journey as it is easy to feel overwhelmed with sensory overload. There's nothing wrong with taking it slow. If Rome wasn't built in a day, neither will your comfort level in new environments.

Instead, a more practical approach is to start with familiar places that interest you. Perhaps you really enjoy art museums, which coincidentally also make for a great date night.

The benefit to doing things that are of interest to you, is that you will likely find other people who share your same interests.

Venture out with friends

When you are with friends there is an inherent sense of security and confidence in social settings. Do yourself a favor and at the very least find a wingman to support you in your quest to finding a date. What you want to avoid is being the person who sits in the corner and looks pathetic.

It's no surprise that dating in a group with friends is hands down one of the best ways to not feel the typical "dating pressure". It's a way to truly feel relaxed and ease the pressure off of finding the "one". You can simply go out, have fun, get the extra boost of confidence to approach a potential date and let the cards fall where they may.

This also gives you an advantage to get a feel of the room for prospective dates at your own leisure. Just as with a wingman, being with a group can help you avoid awkward introductions and break the ice on your behalf. All that's left to do is keep the momentum of the conversation going.

Blind Date Survival Tips

As an introvert, you may be lucky enough to have friends who want to set you up on a blind date. Whenever you're given this opportunity to go on a blind date you should happily accept the offer. Even though after the date it may not evolve into something beyond friendship, which is fine, but you can use the experience to practice and become more comfortable in the dating scene. A blind date can be a hit or miss situation because the premise is usually based upon friends thinking that you and the other person have shared similarities and would get along. However, it can also be the perfect recipe for disaster. Below are a few tips to survive a blind date and to actually have fun!

1. **Remember to be positive!**

You want to go into the blind date feeling confident and with the right mindset that things will go smoothly. Remember, mindset is key to having a wonderful time. The more you let your guard down and allow yourself to have fun, the more enjoyable the experience will be.

2. **Learn about your date**

   It's important to do a little bit of investigative work on your end to discover from friends what your blind date enjoys. Set yourself up for success. If you have met online, feel free to review their online profile again before meeting up so that their interests are fresh and top of mind. Of course, you will have a bit of an advantage if you have already had some dialogue prior to the date.

3. **Select a familiar or comfortable location**

   The more comfortable you both are the higher probability the date will go smoothly. Unfamiliar locations can make for unexpected occurrences and raise anxiety levels through the roof. Familiar territory makes a significant difference in your ability to be at ease and focus more of your attention on what matters most, enjoying your date!

4. **Limit the date to an hour at most**

   Have you ever been on a date and it was going terribly, but you still committed to dinner, a movie and ice cream afterwards? Being stuck with the person for the entire night is one of the worst situations you can be in. Instead, practice what I call the "1 Hour Rule" or "The 1 Drink Maximum Rule".

The idea is simple: Keep things short, sweet and to the point. You want to put the odds in your favor to be able to leave if things are not going smoothly, and this can be achieved easily. When organizing, tell your date that you only have one (1) hour maximum to grab a coffee or a drink because you have other *tentative* obligations.

The keyword here is "*tentative*".

If, after an hour, the date is going well, you can pretend to check in with your friends and tell your date your friends suddenly cancelled plans on you. Alternatively, if things are *not* going well, you have an excuse to leave after an hour. Another approach is to still leave even after an hour has passed. This gives you both an opportunity to reflect on how things went and to plan a "proper" date at a future time. There's no need to rush into things at the beginning stages anyway. It should be noted that this advice does not apply if you have an activity planned for your first date, such as mini golf or bowling, for example.

5. **Be inquisitive**

   Allow the other person to get to you know you and be genuinely curious to learn about them too! Use open-ended questions that cause the person to answer with more than a "yes" or "no".

Whether it's a blind date, with a group of friends or a more "traditional" date with someone who you're familiar with, having confidence is a common theme to ensure things go over as best as they can. It's impossible to predict the outcome of every single situation, but as you can see, there are several ways to maximize the enjoyment for everyone involved.

Chapter 4. The Date

The biggest key to conquering your social confidence as an introvert is to take matters into your own hands. You must be proactive in a way that best fits your personality. The main difference between introverts and extroverts inevitably comes down to what fuels and depletes their energy levels.

For introverts, social settings such as bars, large events, parties and clubs often drain their energy. Instead, they value their alone time often needing to recharge in isolation or quiet environments in smaller groups with close friends.

With this in mind, the traditional advice of throwing yourself out there in night scene doesn't always have to be the answer.

Instead you can take a more proactive approach and seek out activities and environments that still allow you to feel comfortable.

Surprisingly, some of the best ways to meet potential dating prospects is during the day at conferences, meetups and daily interactions. During the day, the mood is different, dating expectations are flipped on its head which allows for more casual and organic interactions. What's more, you'll find that girls' "defensive shields or guards" are often lowered making them a little more approachable. Be proactive about these opportunities and keep your eye open.

I have always found that when I'm actively looking for a date, it never happens when I want. It's better to welcome the idea that a potential prospect could show up in your life when you least expect it, but it's up to you to seize the opportunity and initiate the conversation.

Actionable Tip!

The fear of rejection is worse than the rejection itself. The next time an opportunity presents itself, whether at the museum, the gym, at the grocery store, the library or even someone who catches your eye on the street, ask them out for a cup of coffee or even tea if that's what you prefer. What's the worst that can happen? They say, "No". At the very least you mustered up the courage to ask.

How to ask someone out for coffee and not be creepy

1. Confidence is a highly attractive trait. It's no secret that most girls prefer men who come up to them with a bit of self-confidence. With strong conviction you can easily grab their attention. Start by approaching her with a smile and remember to make direct eye contact. Eye contact is important because it is also a strong indicator of your self-assurance.

2. Pay attention to her body language. Are her arms crossed? Does she make direct eye contact with you? If you smile and she smiles back, this is a good sign that she doesn't feel threatened. Keep a healthy distance between you and her, keeping in mind not to cross into her personal space or uncomfortable territory. One of the ways to be mindful of this is to take a slight, but not aggressive step toward her while in

conversing. If she backs away, you can lean back a bit to maintain the healthy distance.

3. Avoid asking her out for coffee immediately. Instead be yourself, hands at your waist side being calm, cool and collected with an upright posture. To break the ice, you can complement her on what she's wearing or the book she might be reading. Proceed by asking her an open-ended question that allows her to give you a meaningful response and not just a "Yes or no" answer.

4. After a little bit of conversation, you can transition into asking her out. Asking her out for coffee is a casual request, so it doesn't have to be complicated at all. "I would love to learn more about you. There is an excellent coffee place nearby, would you be interested in going sometime either this week or next week?" Regarding timeframe and location, the ask should be flexible but also specific, this week or next week at this place, so that it's easy for her to accept your invitation.

With a proactive mindset you should set goals to meet new people on a weekly basis. Constantly be challenging yourself by attending different events. You want to avoid the "Netflix and chill with yourself" scenario as much as possible. To hold yourself accountable you can either write it down in your journal or have an accountability buddy to help you keep yourself in check. You could even make a deal with your accountability partner to give him or her $100 if you don't make your quota of attending a new event each week.

The more you socialize and push past your comfort zone, the easier it will become to make new connections, have more meaningful conversations and meet potential dates. Start slow with this process, but always remember to leave time for yourself to recharge and gain your energy back. Too much of anything can be stressful and heighten your anxiety.

Date Night!

It's easy to get wrapped up in the belief that "date night" is all about going to bars and being in the social scene or going to a movie where there's a lack of interaction and you aren't able to get to know the person at all. Even worse, bars and getting dinner are often plagued with small talk.

In fact, unless you already know the person, avoid the typical dinner and a movie at all costs!

Thankfully, however, there is an array of a low-key date options for introverts that can make for an enjoyable time, as well. Dates that have some kind of distraction and also have a limited time frame are ideal for introverts.

Here are a few date night ideas to get the creative juices flowing and allow for breaking the ice with ease.

1. **Mini golf**

   Mini golf is a solid option because it's all about having fun. It's not a loud environment, can be just the two of you and also allow you to get to know each other.

2. **Bowling**

Another fun option which allows you both to interact with each other, and build an emotional connection without all of the pressure sitting face to face wondering what to talk about.

3. **Play a board game**

   This is an awesome way to silence the phone, get some food and drinks, and enjoy some friendly competition while getting to know the other person.

4. **Visit an art museum**

   An introvert certainly knows how to appreciate an art museum. They are usually quiet and, if you visit at the right time, the probability of it being crowded is slim. What's more, you both can bond over your love of art in peace and quiet.

5. **Have a Wine & Paint Night**

   The beautiful thing about this idea is that not only is it a fairly commonly offered event throughout a city, but you could also do this at home as well! There's something to be said about letting your guard down, getting creative and sipping on some delicious wine.

These are just a few ideas to make it easier for you and to keep it lighthearted. If you live in an area where Groupon.com or Meetup.com has offerings, this is an easy way to see what fun things are going on in your area. It's normal to feel nervous, and your date probably feels a little nervous as well. So, remember to relax, be playful and try to have fun!

The follow up

The follow up is just as important as the date itself. Often times, we wait too long to follow up and this can send the wrong message. For whatever reason the idea that one should wait at least three days after the date before contacting the other again has become popular. I'm going to tell you right now that is an awful idea.

If you were vibing with the other person and you are genuinely interested in hanging out again, then avoid making them guess how you feel. Dating is stressful enough and to be left in the dark sucks. Take the time to send a thoughtful message the evening of the following day, at the very latest.

The text can be as simple as:

"Hi (name), I really enjoyed hanging out with you today / tonight. I'd like to get to know you better if you'd be interested."

Easy peasy, right? A simple message will not only convey that you had a nice time, but will give the opportunity for the other person to express their feelings and give light on whether they are interested in hanging out again.

On the other hand, if you don't feel the date went well or that you're not compatible with each other do NOT make any future plans. Too often people will string along the other person out of pure boredom or out of fear hurting someone's feelings. It's better to take the approach or "hell yes!" or "no". If you're feeling lukewarm or not 100% about spending another second with that person it's a simple, "no". This takes out the guesswork and the indecisiveness, not to mention making a final decision is a breath of fresh air.

Don't worry, as the saying goes, "there are plenty of fish in the sea." You will be happier in the long run by being patient and spending your energy and efforts on someone you are compatible with.

Conclusion

On its face, dating can be a finicky and overwhelming experience, but with the right mindset and patience you will find it less and less daunting. There's no better feeling than finding someone you can share your life. In the end, the struggles you inevitably will face will all be worth it. Take time to review these chapters again and let this powerful advice marinate. The only thing holding you back from breaking down the mental barriers is confronting your limiting beliefs head on. Use each day to its fullest and take each failure as a blessing to become more confident in yourself and approach. Be true to yourself and know that before you can fully be happy and love someone else unconditionally, you need to first love yourself.

It's time to take massive action and create the life you deserve!

Good luck.

Book 4.

Public Speaking

Simple, Effective Methods and Strategies to Overcome Shyness, Build Confidence, Increase Persuasion and Become Excellent at Public Speaking

Introduction

When we hear the words "Public Speaking" the first thing that comes to mind is a graduation speech or a politician addressing the crowd as part of their campaign, maybe an actor thanking their fans after receiving an award. On a personal level, it may mean giving a presentation at school or at work. Furthermore, the image we have of a public speaker is someone articulate and confident with an impeccable appearance, a leader of sorts. Unless our profession requires us to speak frequently in public, it is quite uncommon to find ourselves in a situation where we will have to address a crowd. We go on through life, believing that public speaking is not a beneficial skill and ultimately something that we don't need to learn. However, the least that can be said about this mindset is that it is limited and wrong.

While the majority of the people think of public speaking as the formal act of communicating information in front of a live audience, in reality, it is in nearly every situation that requires us to address a group of people in order to inform them about something and to influence them in some way. That may still sound like something only leaders would need to do, but it is not.

Public speaking is not exclusive to people who have to master it as a part of their profession; literally anyone might need to speak in public at any given time.

You might need to give a speech at your best friend's wedding, public speaking skills would be a very important set of tools to possess in order to deliver beautiful and moving words at an important event in the life of one of the closest people to you. Addressing a crowd at a moment like that without those skills can quickly turn into an embarrassing experience to both you and your best friend. Another example of public speaking is fund raisers. There might be a time in your life when you will need to raise money for a cause and at that time, you will want to speak in a way that tells the people you are addressing just how important that particular cause is to you and just how passionate you are about it. Your passion will shine through enough to move them into adopting such a cause themselves and donating for its benefit.

You must have noticed when attending an event or while watching a recording of a great public speaker, how they motivate you to take action and inspire you to make a change, it is like they are oozing confidence and charisma. Everything they say is uplifting as well as how they say it. They do it in a way that seems effortless and you might even think that it comes naturally to them and while that may be true for some, in most cases, public speaking is an art that they had to learn and invest time and effort into.

Mastering public speaking not only helps you build confidence and learn how to express yourself eloquently, it improves your communication skills and teaches you how to convincingly argue a point. In today's world, communication skills truly matter to solve problems, pass along knowledge and make progress in various aspects of life.

Public speaking is something that would make or break a person's career in the business world. For example, when businesspeople have an idea that they would like to turn into a project, they have to pitch it. That means that they have to argue the benefits that the project would yield and why it would be a profitable investment. Not only that, public speaking also helps them attract customers and increase sales. They have to do this often, practicing and honing their public speaking skills all the time, increasing their confidence as they have to sound sure of themselves.

If you still think public speaking is not your scene, think of your friends who have to do some sort of public speaking as part of their job. They usually are the first to jump in and lead a game or an activity at a get together and they do it well, hyping up the whole group and turning the outing into a fun adventure whether you all gathered to grab pizza at the local fast food parlor or on a camping trip, they are fun, confident and clever and everyone admires them. They also are great at getting to know people, always making new friends and connections, they make networking seem easy.

Public speaking is a highly sought-after skill in the workplace, mainly because employers want people who can represent the company well and not just at formal marketing events, they know that an opportunity to expand can present itself at any time and they want the person present to be able to cease it. Not only that, but actors, singers, writers all have to master public speaking as they have to promote their work and attend conferences where they have to speak of their last release, so it really isn't just about business and politics.

Even famous YouTubers attend events like Comic Con and interact with their followers.

Though public speaking is so beneficial, to some people, the idea of it is just terrifying due to a fear of performing in front of a large crowd or speaking to people in general. However, whether you suffer from that kind of anxiety or are perfectly comfortable addressing strangers but lack the polish to do it, this book has what you need to help you master public speaking. You, as well, can become as good as a professional by learning how public speaking works and what would take your public speaking to a different level and practicing it often.

Though there are some skills out there that are hard to obtain, public speaking really isn't one of them. You have everything you need to develop and master this craft and use it to make your life even more interesting. Once you have mastered it, public speaking can open doors you had no idea even existed and will enable you to enjoy incredible new experiences. This book's main goal is to help you get to that point, it teaches you how public speaking works and gives you tips and tricks to take it to the next level. Mastering public speaking is beneficial in an array of ways as it promotes self-discovery, enables self-expression and ultimately builds confidence.

Effective communication is considered the key anchor in navigating society because it can be used to influence decisions, instill change and form lifelong connections.

What are you waiting for? Dig into the next pages and start absorbing the knowledge that will make you a better public speaker. You can be that person who speaks motivational words to the masses and gets the crowd excited to try new things. You have the power to become a business person who will convince investors to support a revolutionary project or even the best man or woman who gives a killer speech at a wedding. The ball is in your court now!

CHAPTER 1. UNDERSTANDING THE IMPORTANCE OF PUBLIC SPEAKING

When you have to speak in public, it is very important for you to know the context of your speech. Who will you be addressing? What will you talk about? How will you deliver the points you will be making? These are some of the questions you should be asking yourself in the preparation phase. Keep in mind that you will not just be there to speak and be heard. You want these people to listen to your ideas and adopt them for themselves. You want their support. You want them to hear you and cling to your every word. After all, these people came to your event expecting to gain something from you. Once you know how to do it, get the crowd fired up can become one of the greatest things you have done in your life.

Public speaking has two main phases to it:

1. Preparation phase
2. Execution phase

The execution phase happens when you get up there and start talking. The preparation phase is everything that happens before that. When done correctly, the two phases will result in a great speech in which you would have effectively communicated all your thoughts and ideas. If one of the phases is lacking, the speech will most likely fail.

Think about it this way, if you have a great topic to speak about and a flawlessly written speech, will it be a success if you cannot convey it properly? On the other hand, it doesn't matter how much spirit you can pump into your speech if it's hollow to begin with. If you talk about things that don't matter, people will simply not care enough to remember them. While you would have succeeded in engaging their attention, you would have failed at making an impact.

Understanding the Context:

Public speaking is a tool that is used in practically every field. Whether you need to give a presentation at school, exhibit a project to potential clients or even convincing your neighbors to adopt kittens from the shelter you volunteer at. Understanding the context of your speech can help you choose the right approach to go about it. You cannot talk about profits and gains when talking about a little kitten, can you? You have more chances of finding a home for the little feline by talking about how cute it is and how much warmth a person can get from taking care of a pet.

Another aspect of understanding the context is understanding your audience. In order to engage the audience, you have to be certain that you will speak about something that interests them. The people who will be listening to you have to be willing to grant you their attention and ready to engage with you. Doing your research about your audience beforehand will help pick the right words and say them in a more meaningful way to garner interest when you speak, resulting in a more receptive audience.

Be Authentic:

In other words, be yourself. You are a unique person with unique qualities, know how to play those qualities to your advantage when delivering your speech and it will turn out great. Furthermore, being yourself while you are the center of attention will help you become more confident as you know you are doing this as yourself and not some fake façade that you will shed once the speech is over. Your movements will also be more consistent with what you are saying as you will be acting naturally. Don't try to imitate the style of famous public speakers, their movements and manner of speech work best for them and may ruin your speech if you perform them awkwardly. You do not want your audience to be distracted by your antics while they should be focusing on your words.

Master Your Topic:

Picking a great topic is a critical first step start, what you have to do next is research. Understanding your topic will not only help you write an amazing speech, it will also come in handy when you forget parts of your speech as you will be able to reformulate and express the main idea differently; or in case you are asked questions after the speech. When you have a strong understanding of something you will inevitably become more comfortable speaking about it as you are confident that you know what you are talking about. You are in your element and once you start speaking, you can focus on the delivery rather than the content.

Improvise When Needed:

Improvising might be an intimidating prospect to some people when speaking publicly but sometimes it can be your only option in the event things don't go according to plan. While you might be in full control of your subject, content and performance, there will always be things beyond your control such as the stage, electronic technical difficulties and the most unpredictable variable of all: the audience. A problem that is unaccounted for can arise at any moment. It could be a power shortage causing a loss of key projected data you rely on to help the audience understand what you are talking about, a sudden downpour on stage that was set outside or even an unexpected question or comment from someone in the audience. No matter what it is, stay calm and think of a way to work through that problem. You can use a white board and markers to present the lost data, ask the staff to close the door to help your voice carry better and relocate to somewhere dry to counter the rain problem. As for tough questions, there is no shame in asking them to reformulate the question so that you can understand it better. If you have done your research properly, you will have a strong grasp on the subjects and a better chance of fielding unexpected questions that may arise.

Flaunt Your Strong Points:

We all are different and have unique qualities. Some of us are spirited and can bring cheer and excitement to a room, others know how to tell an engaging story and can capture the audience's interest easily and there are those who are highly passionate and it shows in the way they talk and move. It doesn't matter which one you are, there is more than one way to breathe life into a crowd, you just need to know what your strengths are and use them to your advantage in order to connect with your audience and deliver a powerful speech. If you don't know what your strengths are, ask the people around you. Those who know you best such as friends and colleagues will be able to instantly share with you your strengths as well as your areas that could use some improvement. Simply ask them to spend some time with you, so you can rehearse your speech with them and gain positive and constructive feedback.

CHAPTER 2. THE IMPORTANCE OF BUILDING CONFIDENCE

In order to deliver a speech that not only resonates with the audience, but keeps them engaged it's extremely important to have confidence. This is also the case in public speaking. When giving a speech in front of an audience, it is important to communicate that you believe in what you are saying and you are sure of yourself. Confidence also helps your speech go smoothly as you perform with full trust in your public speaking abilities, you know you are doing things correctly and you have a strong grasp on the subject at hand. Confidence, at the very least, will help you appear as if everything is under your control.

Not feeling confident may have resulted from a lack of education or perhaps there was no importance given to this trait while you were young and therefore you never were afforded the opportunity to develop it. It may also have been caused by something that happened which took a toll on your self-esteem, perhaps you were ignored while speaking or told to quiet down when you felt you have something of importance to say. To build confidence, you must be ready to let go of whatever happened in the past and change your way of thinking. Confidence is a feeling, a state of mind and in order to build it up, you have to convince yourself of your own self-worth. You also have to change your attitude towards failure and start seeing it as a motivator to try harder.

Being a confident public speaker means that you can go through your speech without showing signs of fear or nervousness. The people listening to you will see a calm and composed individual who are sure of what they are saying. In order to achieve this, you have to deal with what makes you nervous and overcome it and not just push away the nerves and pretend they are not there. Once on the stage, you might be overwhelmed by the amount of people facing you and all those feelings you kept at bay will flood your senses all at the same time. Confidence is not a lack of fear, it is an ability to face that fear and deal with it properly so that it becomes an asset instead of a shortcoming.

You can rely on the following steps to overcome your fear and increase your confidence ...

Embrace a Positive Mental Image:

Having a positive perception of oneself is one of the key ingredients of confidence. It is often what we think of ourselves that brings us down the most, if you think you are a failure, it will be very hard for anyone to break you out of that mindset but if you think you are a winner, no amount of people telling you otherwise will affect you.

Here is how you can develop a better mental image:

- Imagine yourself speaking in public, better yet, have a rehearsal with a few friends acting as your audience and take note of which of your senses are the most alert, what you feel as you are speaking and why you feel that way. Do you feel nervous? Afraid? Confident? Excited? How are these feelings related to your perception of yourself?

- When you imagine yourself speaking, how close are you to your audience? Do you feel more comfortable when they are farther from you? Do you feel a better connection when you are positioned closer to the people who are present? Try to simulate these situations in your rehearsal with your friends, ask them to pull their chairs closer or farther and see what distance you are most comfortable with and makes you feel the most confident.

- If someone in the audience bothers you because they are not paying attention or rolling your eyes at you, picture them with silly cat ears or imagine that they are sitting in a stroller instead of a chair, this might sound counterintuitive but by doing so, the overwhelming feeling of anxiety and your nerves will be put to ease.

- Pay attention to the audience. If they are silent, they are paying attention to you, if they are laughing after you made a joke to lighten the mood, they are in tune and engaged with you. Their reactions to your speech can help you keep going and boost your confidence.

Visualizing Public Speaking Success:

Whenever you imagine yourself speaking in public, imagine that you are doing it confidently. If you believe that you aren't confident, it will show in your performance and your speech will be ruined. Your thoughts directly influence your performance, therefore putting yourself in the right positive mental state will help you significantly when you are facing the crowd.

Here is how you can visualize your success while speaking in public:

1. Breathing exercises have always been a great way to effectively manage nervousness and anxiety. Close your eyes, take a deep breath and exhale slowly. Just imagine, while you are breathing, you are inhaling a cloud of confidence and exhaling one of fear and nerves.

2. Picture the audience's reaction to what you say. Imagine yourself speaking confidently and imagine them watching you in awe, hanging onto your every word. They are impressed and are greatly enjoying your speech.

3. After you say the closing words of your speech, exit the frame of mind you had when you were talking and think back to how confident and empowered you were as you delivered your speech. Look at how pleased the audience is with your performance as they give you a round of applause.

4. Rely on these visualization techniques every time you have to speak in public to build up your confidence.

Recognize and Destroy the Inner Critic:

As humans we tend to be our own worst critics and that is a fact. No doubt you are very hard on yourself and whenever you fail, you keep replaying your mistakes and reprimanding yourself over and over in a vicious never-ending cycle of negative, self-deprecating thoughts. Sometimes, they don't stem from your shortcomings but from harsh words other people have said to you; words that might have been said to you out of jealousy and are probably not even be true.

These negative thoughts can damage your self-esteem if you believe them and don't stop them when they occur. These are the thoughts that we refer to as the inner critic.

To overcome these negative thoughts and "slay the inevitable inner critic" below are some simple tips you can start implementing right now.

Focus on the Wins:

Think back to your successful moments when speaking in public as many or as few as they are.

This will encourage you to keep going as you will be aware that you have managed to make it through those instances. The fact that you've garnered a positive response from the audience will also boost your confidence.

Replace the Bad with the Good:

Interrupt the negative dialogue that runs in your head and start thinking positive thoughts instead. A good strategy is to think of two (or more) positive thoughts for every negative thought you have about yourself.

Use a Persona:

Though it isn't advised to imitate others or "faking it" when you deliver your speech, developing a stage persona can help you overcome the nerves and anxiety and tap into the more confident side of yourself. An alter ego of sorts. Someone who you can become when you are speaking in public. Some entertainers do it and you can see the difference between who they really are when they speak in talk shows and who they become on stage and it is simply incredible how much more confident and charismatic they become.

Here is how to develop your very own fearless stage persona:

- Identify your best features as a public speaker. Resilience, compassion, coolness, it can be anything or any number of things. Focus on those features and use them to flesh out your persona.

- Pay attention to your movements and body language as you speak. Do you talk with your hands a lot? Do you stay still? Do you pace around the stage? Identify your pattern and use it to become a stronger, more confident version of yourself on stage.

A Balanced Mix:

To become an accomplished public speaker, you should seek to have a perfect balance between confidence and certainty. You are the one responsible for maintaining that balance as no one has the ability to overcome your fears for you. You are the one charged with practicing your public speaking skills and improving them as you go.

You can become confident if you firmly believe in yourself and once you do no one can take that away from you.

Daily Positive Affirmations for Public Speaking Mastery

Affirmations are an effective way to release negative emotions and reinforce positive ones. Emotions which are not accepted represents an aspect of the self that is being judged. These emotions cause sensations in the body that you either yearn for or have an aversion to. Repeating affirmations are also an excellent tool to help reinforce positive messages and instill confidence.

Feel free to repeat the phrases below in the mirror several times in the morning and before going to sleep. You'll be surprised how much of a lasting impact this can be to build up your confidence.

List of Affirmations for Public Speaking Mastery

1. Today, I am fearless.
2. I am grateful for this opportunity to connect with others.
3. Speaking to this audience, I find myself becoming energized and excited.
4. I connect with the audience so naturally.
5. My message is so important, and the audience wants to receive it.
6. I enjoy hearing the sound of my own voice.
7. I love presenting and sharing my ideas.
8. My words have a lasting and positive effect on other people.
9. I can't wait to practice this new skill of public speaking!
10. I am a powerful, courageous and inspiring speaker.
11. I am more and more comfortable speaking in front of others.
12. I'm sincere with my words and going to have great results.
13. Today, I expect success.

"You gain strength, courage, and confidence by every experience in which you really stop to look fear in the face. You are able to say to yourself, 'I lived through this horror. I can take the next thing that comes along." **-Eleanor Roosevelt**

Chapter 3. Speech Creation and Delivery

As stated before, being skilled at crafting and delivering a speech are the two main elements which make a great public speaker.

Creating a speech is what was referred to previously as the preparation phase. It is all the research and data gathering, the outlining and planning of the speech as well as the proper organization to ensure it has good idea flow. All of this is needed to write a memorable speech. After this is done, you can move on to the delivery phase, or the execution phase as mentioned earlier.

The delivery phase is what determines if you are a good speaker or not. While you deliver your content to an audience, all your positive features come into play. Your confidence shines through as you speak and your mastery of the subject is reflected in your ability to eloquently communicate the information in a meaningful and impactful way. This is what shows your audience that you came well prepared and know what you are talking about. It is also in this phase in which any lack of preparation or residual nervousness can catch up with you, which is why it is important to be prepared as much as possible.

Actionable Tips

Here is what you need to do to create your speech:

Research and preparation:

Make sure you do some research about your audience:

- Where are they from?
- What is their age group?
- What is their cultural background?

Ask yourself these things as they might be relevant to your speech and will help you connect with the crowd. Once that is solidified, use the appropriate tone of speech and deliver the right information. Try to think of yourself as a part of the audience and think about what you would want to get out of this speech. What are your expectations?

It is also necessary to thoroughly research your topic. Gather as much information as possible and understand every single word you are going to use. This is very important as it would be quite embarrassing if you are asked about the meaning of a word you used and couldn't answer because you don't know it yourself.

Overcome Anxiety:

It is very common for symptoms of anxiety to arise during a public speech. Those can come in the form of rapid breathing, shaky limbs, excessive sweating, stuttering and many other things. This, clearly, can directly interfere with a proper delivery of your speech as you will be in no condition to speak powerfully. What's more, your audience could become too distracted by your anxious state causing them to not be able to focus on your speech and intended message, which obviously would be a bad thing.

That is not to say you should not be feeling any fear before speaking publicly, but rather that you should control that fear and any feelings of apprehension. Use these emotions to power through your speech and motivate yourself to do the best you can. A feeling of failure, for instance, will push you to be well prepared and that nervous energy can be converted into positive energy you can use to hype up the crowd.

Write Your Speech

Planning what you will say is of the highest importance if you want your speech to go smoothly. A well written opening can set the tone of your speech and capture your audience' interest. Then smoothly transition to the body of your speech. Once you are all done, a carefully written closing statement that sums up your speech will make for a beautiful finish.

Here are a few tips to help you write your speech:

- **Make your introduction as interesting as possible:** You can do that by stating a fascinating fact or using a quote, an anecdote or even a question. The goal here is to capture your audience' attention quickly before they deem you uninteresting and lose interest.

- **Be positive:** A smile, a bright tone, a clear-sounding voice and an energetic body language will keep the audience interested.

- **Implicate the audience:** If possible, when delivering your speech, do it in a way that makes the audience feel directly concerned. State the problem and solution in a way that makes them feel that they are actions that they can take to make a change.

- Strong conclusion: Just as the intro was supposed to grab the audience' attention, the closure should make sure they are impacted by your speech. You can't get lazy at this point! Summarize all that you have spoken about and end the speech with a powerful call to action. Your conclusion must inspire the audience to take some sort of action.

Practice, Practice, Practice

Saying your words repeatedly in different ways can help you find the right tone of speech you want to go for. Rehearsing in front of people you know can make speaking in front of a crowd of strangers a less daunting prospect and practicing your delivery will help you get a firmer grasp of your topic. This last point is because practicing will make your performance more natural as you will be talking about things you know instead of parroting words you memorized.

Rehearse your speech as many times as you need to feel confident enough that you could recite it from heart.

You can start by practicing in your empty room, then in front of a mirror. After that, having a friend around to listen to you can help you catch the little mistakes that you may have missed after being exposed to your speech for a long time. If possible, increase the number of people listening to you each new round of practice, as it will not only simulate your future audience, but will gradually help you get used to performing in front of people.

Mastering pacing and gestures can serve as a way to help you let out nervous energy and add more character to your speech. Movement is more interesting than standing still in the same position. Making eye contact is also very important to remember as it allows the audience to feel a connection with you on an individual basis.

Actionable Tip

> *If making eye contact makes you nervous, look at the top of people's heads to give off the illusion of eye contact. However, make sure to shift your gaze regularly to make it appear as if you are looking at different people.*

It is also important to incorporate these movements to your rehearsal as you will want people to tell you if a particular gesture you do seems too quirky or unnatural.

Set the Tone

The meaning of tone here is the general mood you want to set throughout your speech. Your tone of voice, on the other hand, reflects your level of confidence, your current state of mind and your attitude which can help you set the mood. You can come across as strong, charming, relatable or anything else when you use the right tone of voice. Often times, the tone is set by the nature of the event you are speaking at, such as at a graduation, for instance. You can set the tone before you even start talking through your facial expressions and the way you carry yourself. For example, if you are speaking about something that is supposed to be inspiring, a bright smile will communicate you are a friendly, inviting person who is there to give useful advice. If you are going to speak about global warming, a serious expression and a firm voice will tell your listeners that this is a serious and urgent matter.

Language Style

This is the pace you set for your speech, the pitch of your voice and your volume. How clear and precise your speech is also included in your style. Using formal and informal speech accordingly is also important and should be compatible with the occasion.

Do not use overly complicated language and rely on metaphors and similes to better carry your point. Do not speak too fast nor too slow and be sure to make necessary, yet natural pauses.

Use Visual Aids

This includes PowerPoint slides, pictures, charts, videos and any supporting evidence that will better illustrate to your audience key information so they can easily follow along to your speech.

When preparing visual aids, keep them simple and clear. Use contrast for better visibility and make sure any writing is legible to your audience but, limit your texts to titles, as you do not want your audience to shift their attention to reading the visual aids instead of listening to what you are saying. As their name suggests, they are supposed to help you in your speech not distract your audience from it.

Handling Q&A

Answering your audience's questions can be a great way for you to demonstrate your mastery of the topic. They will find you more credible as you answer the questions confidently, clarifying anything that was ambiguous in the speech or expanding on ideas that you couldn't explore further because of the time limitation.

It is always a good idea to anticipate questions you could potentially be asked and be prepared to give thorough answers. Your friends can also help you with this in the rehearsals.

In case anyone becomes antagonistic or persistent and it feels like they are hijacking your presentation in the Q&A session, tell them that you are open to exploring the matter further at a later time as you would like to address as many questions as possible before the end of the presentation.

Vocal Preparation

This mainly pertains to the variety in your tone, the pauses you make as you speak and the speaking rate. You should have variation in your speech as sounding the same throughout the whole talk can sound monotonous and boring. The intonation in your voice and the variations in your vocals are what will keep your audience interested and most importantly always make sure you are speaking loud enough to be heard by everyone.

"You are the only person on earth who can use your ability." **– Zig Ziglar**

CHAPTER 4. PUBLIC SPEAKING MASTERY WITH 10 SIMPLE STRATEGIES

While the main goal of learning public speaking is to gain the ability to give inspiring speeches, it has other advantages, like improving yourself in business dealings. It also makes you better able to clearly communicate your thoughts and argue your points more convincingly.

Follow these simple tips to master public speaking:

Unleash the Inner Master:

To excel at public speaking, you must mobilize your mind and body. Having the right mindset and the behaviors to back it up will make you sound and look more natural as well as give you credibility as a speaker. Doing all the right things but lacking the right attitude will be evident in your performance and the incoherence will harm your speech.

Being confident and believing that your topic will add value to your listeners' lives is the basis you need to start from. From there, you can fine tune the skills necessary to improve your delivery such as body language, cadence, eye contact and vocals.

Practice the Art of Storytelling:

Stories and tales have fascinated human beings since the beginning of time. We are naturally curious and enjoy a good plot. We love the feeling of suspense and anticipation and are always itching to know what happens next. Great speakers know how to use this tendency to their advantage. They know that people tend to remember a story they heard decades ago more than a fact they learned a few years back. Which is why they incorporate storytelling to their speeches.

In order for you to do the same, make sure that your story is simple and relatable. You want your audience to connect with the characters and to get the point of the tale easily. If you can make it personal, go for it! It will add credibility to your speech and inspire your audience.

Remember that you are sharing your experience for the benefit of the audience so focus on what can help them or guide them in some way. Avoid becoming sidetracked by getting too caught up in irrelevant details.

Your story doesn't have to be too long, you can also use parts of it or anecdotes to help make certain points clearer and more impactful in your speech.

Focus on the audience and ignite a conversation

When addressing the audience, keep in mind that you are not addressing one single entity but a group of unique individuals. Everyone came to your presentation expecting to connect with you in some way and be impacted by what you will say. Every single person would like to gain something from the experience of hearing you speak. Making eye contact with different people in the audience, speaking deliberately and making sure that your focus is on satisfying the audience rather than coming across as an accomplished speaker will establish the needed connection with your listeners.

Deliver captivating moments

Being genuine and speaking from the heart will help you keep it real with the audience. These people want to listen to a real human share their experience with them. Moving your audience emotionally through an intense story or by making them laugh with a light-hearted anecdote will add substance to your presentation and add the human factor to what would otherwise be just a bunch of facts and instructions. Make sure you use the right tone of voice and gestures to breathe life into your speech and reflect the proper emotion.

Grab Attention and Close with a Dynamic Ending

Impressions are formed very quickly, people judge how your presentation will go by your first sentences without even realizing it. They can deem you interesting enough or not in the first few moments. Which is why the opening of your speech is very important because it will either bore your audience to the point of making them lose interest or grab their attention and engage their focus.

To capture the crowd's attention, start your speech with something interesting like a quote a question or a story. Do not waste time thanking the host or sponsors or fiddling with the technicalities of turning your computer on and displaying your visual aids, those should be done beforehand.

Once you make it to the closure of your speech, it is always a good idea to sum things up and briefly go over the main points of your presentation. Pair that up with a strong and inspiring call to action which directs your audience to do a specific task.

The 20 Minute Rule

A well-crafted speech can evoke emotion and pack a ton of information into a small period of time. For this very reason, a good time limit for a speech is 20 minutes so as to not inundate or overwhelm the audience. The more you say, the more difficult it is to process, internalize and remember it all. If you have to speak for more than 20 minutes, try to make the presentation interactive to engage and captivate the audience. This can be done by allowing them to ask questions after a certain section or asking them for their input. Speakers often ask questions like, "Who here has ever...?" Or "Which of you believe that...?" and the audience would answer by raising their hands.

Engage all the 5 senses

The more senses you engage in a person, the more alert they become to incoming stimuli and information. This can be very useful to capture your audience's attention throughout a speech.

Visual aids, eye contact and body language are very effective when it comes to engaging eyesight.

Playing music at certain points of the presentation and using your vocals properly engage the hearing. Asking questions and allowing the audience to reflect on what you say can engage their thoughts. Shaking hands, touching someone's shoulder or high-fiving someone from the audience would engage the sense of touch and asking them to repeat empowering words will engage speech.

Study the Masters

What better way to learn than to mimic experts in a field? You can pick up many things from watching presentations of expert public speakers and following their footsteps. While imitation is highly discouraged, getting inspired from your favorite speaker can be very useful. Some of those speakers even share their tricks and secrets through social media to help you become a better speaker. So, do not hesitate to research them and learn from them.

Let Your Personality Shine Through

Staying true to yourself and not imitating others will allow you to develop your own unique style. Your passion, energy and authenticity will be reflected in your speech. Speaking from the heart, mastering your topic and believing in your message will shine through to your audience and it will give you more credibility. Your audience will be more likely to trust you enough to make a connection when they perceive that you are being yourself and keeping it real with them.

Fully Embrace Failure

Embrace failure and stop seeing it as a negative thing. Some things can only be learned by getting them wrong the first time and learning from that failure.

You can also use failure as a source of motivation and push yourself to get back up and work harder to succeed.

Failure will also allow you to appreciate the success that comes after and help you remember not to take it for granted.

And no matter what, never let a failure or a fear of failure keep you from going out there and putting your public speaking skills to practice. You will never improve if you don't take risks and stay in the confines of your comfort zone.

"Failure is a great teacher, and I think when you make mistakes and you recover from them and you treat them as valuable learning experiences, then you've got something to share." **-Steve Harvey**

CHAPTER 5. DEVELOPING & MASTERING PERSUASION SKILLS

Having persuasion skills means having the ability to convince people through argument, changing their mind about something or having them adopt a concept or an idea that they were indifferent about before. This involves the ability to direct and guide people, appealing to their reason and challenging their already existing thoughts. The end goal is to have the audience accept the ideas shared in the speech.

In order to persuade your audience, you should first know them and understand them. Knowing what their needs and expectations are will enable you to answer to those needs and fulfil those expectations. A good way to do that is to put yourself in their shoes and try to see things from their perspective. What would your expectations be if you were a part of the audience? Focus on that and think of how you can best satisfy the audience.

You can improve your persuasive skills through three elements;

Ethos:

This is a Greek word that means "character". In a public speaking context, we mean the character of the speaker and their credibility. You must express some level of authority and confidence that reflects your mastery of the subject you speak of in order to inspire trust in your audience. For that it is important that you garner respect from your audience. The fact that you are of good character and trustworthy should be established and you should be viewed as an authority in the subject you are speaking in. Once your audience view you as someone like that, they are more open to what you will be saying and you can work on persuading them.

Logos:

As the word may suggest, this aspect is relative to the logic behind your arguments and anything else you might say. Human beings rely on reasoning in various aspects of life and if they are more likely to be persuaded by what you say if they perceive it as logical. To establish this, make sure that your speech makes sense and is free of incoherence. It is important that what you say is backed up by facts, evidence, studies and statistics.

Pathos:

In Greek, this word means "emotion". It is your ability to make a connection with the audience and move their emotions. This will enable you to better capture the audience's attention and hold their interest. You can establish an emotional connection by using similes, metaphors and analogies or through sharing your personal experiences by telling a story. The aim is to trigger a certain feeling that would then inspire the listener to take action. Be aware of the emotion your words and tone of voice inspire and use them to your advantage.

How to Be Persuasive in 3 Simple Steps:

Trying to influence someone can be a very tricky process, and even more so when it's a crowd of people who all have different opinions and experiences shaping their views.

In a simple 3 step process you can not only keep an audience engaged, but deliver your message in a meaningful and impactful way.

Step 1. Grab their attention

You only have a few seconds to set the tone and capture your audience's attention, which is why starting off strong is important.

A. **Start with the unexpected:** Listeners love presentations that spark interest quickly with the first sentence.

   "I wish you could have been there..." -Patricia Fripp, CSP, Former President of the National Speakers Association.

This opening line creates engagement and makes us wanting to hear more about what will happen next. Suspense, curiosity and intrigue should be included in your speech to make it as engaging as possible right from the start.

B. **Make it all about them:** After capturing their attention with your impactful opening, make the story about them. Always keep your audience in mind as to their aspirations, what their struggles are and their goals. If you simply remind an audience of their pain points, a threat to their livelihood or a felt need you will always keep them engaged.

C. **Get straight to the point:** Often times we like to add fluff to speeches or go on tangents with irrelevant information before actually getting to the intended point.

Step 2. Create a connection

The goal of creating a connection is to make them think, "This relates to my life and it is easy enough for me to do."

If it's not relevant to my life, you've lost me. If it's too complicated, you've lost me. I can't fix global warming, but I can cast a vote. Connect your message to me (especially through storytelling), and you've got a chance.

If you want a standing chance at truly persuading your audience then you need to figure out how it will be relevant to their life. If the speech or concept is too complicated, you risk the chance of losing their interest and attention.

Think of global warming. An audience may not know the impact of it on their lives, however once they see the relevance and know they have the power to fix it through taking a stand at the voting polls their interest is piqued. Through clever storytelling you can evoke emotion and persuade nearly anyone to take a stand on a topic.

A. **Evoke emotion:** Humor is one of the most effective ways to persuade an audience due to its ability to change the mood and chemistry in the room. If you're not a comedian, do not go overboard with jokes because then your audience may not take you seriously. What's better, in fact, is to simply be yourself and allow your natural sense of humor shine through with a joke here and there. If an opportunity arises to make a small joke or to lighten the mood, allow it come out naturally, but never force humor or jokes in your speech.

   Additionally, when you let your guard down and reveal that you too are simply human with vulnerabilities the audience can relate and feel connected to you. Do not feel embarrassed to share personal stories because as humans we actually remember those far better than factual information.

B. **Be interactive:** Studies have shown that an engaged audience that interacts are more easily persuaded than a passive audience. This has been demonstrated throughout time in churches during worship, school and universities where students are asked to participate in answering questions and even rallies for a moral cause or purpose.

Step 3. Encourage them to take massive action

More often than not, we are scared to ask for what we want. Just as the saying goes, "Closed mouths don't get fed." When you are direct and tell them to take a specific action, less confusion arises and that action is followed.

Up until this point, you have been grooming your audience to feel a certain way. After you have instilled these emotions, go in for the ask.

Again, stories are a great way to exemplify and allow the audience to see from your point of view. Use a powerful closing story that is in alignment with how you want them to feel hours after your speech. If you want them to feel excited, share an enthusiastic and energetic story.

Conclusion

You've made it to the end of the book! Congratulations!

Thank you for choosing this book and reading it until the last word. Now that you have the necessary knowledge, take action and practice what you have learned to become a great public speaker.

Follow the steps and take massive action whenever you get the chance. The more you practice the better you will get. Make sure to keep track of your progress because there are things that you can only learn by experience. Remember, failure is a powerful tool that can help you achieve your goals. When failure does come, embrace it because it happens to the best of us. Facing these obstacles is a part of the learning process so welcome your mistakes and learn from them. Just keep up your momentum and you will see the results before you know it.

There is no time to lose! Get out there and make unforgettable speeches that inspire people to become the best version of themselves!

Book 5.

Confidence

Easy, Proven Strategies to Effectively Manage Shyness and Anxiety to Transform Your Professional and Personal Life

INTRODUCTION

Imagine what it would be like if you could fearlessly enter into a conversation in any situation. How would your life change if you had the confidence to overcome your shyness and command the attention of a room effortlessly?

Since the beginning of time, confidence has been a dominant trait that characterizes the strong and accomplished. People see someone confident and think this is a fearless person, a leader, a pioneer. Confident people are perceived as these human beings who always know what they want, are sure of themselves and can do no wrong. This might be partly true for some of those people but for the most part, this perception is due to the pedestal that we, ourselves, put confident people on. In truth, they are people just like us, susceptible to feelings of fear and nervousness and just as capable of making mistakes. The only difference is that they have trained themselves to face fear head on.

It is a common misconception that confident people are simply born with an overabundance of confidence. That a person is either confident or not. But that is just not the case.

While some people grew up in households that elevated their self-esteem, causing them to develop "natural" confidence, a lot of people learn it by conscious choice and hard work to achieve it.

When you look up the meaning of confidence, you will find most definitions say it is the certainty in one's ability to succeed and one's belief in themselves. An absence of self-doubt, if you will.

The feeling of self-assurance and creating a solid belief in one's self takes time, but can ultimately be learned with persistence. You can learn how to fully place trust in your abilities and how to silence the feelings of doubt and uncertainty when they arise. You can even change the way you feel about yourself because your feelings are yours to control. You simply just need to know how to do it.

Confidence is a very desirable trait. It reflects how determined you are to succeed and how much you believe in your vision. It shows how steadfast you can be when facing obstacles and that you have enough courage to overcome your fears. It is a valuable asset in communication and leadership. It enables you to make important decisions and to follow through with them. It can feel like an uphill battle mustering up confidence, but the reality is that half the job is already done when you have absolute faith in your own abilities. People naturally gravitate towards those who exude confidence as it inspires trust. Simply put, people like to follow someone who knows where they are going.

There's no doubt that the most successful people in life are the "go-getters". Those who are not afraid to take risks and always shoot for the stars because they strongly believe they only deserve the best.

Once you become confident in yourself, you are practically bulletproof. No amount of criticism, taunting or negativity can stand in your way because you know who you are and what you are capable of. Everything else is irrelevant.

Confidence is such a powerful tool. If you are confident, people believe you, brings success, helps to create strong bonds with others and you feel happier overall. The only one who can say you're not confident is you.

The fear of asking your boss for a raise will seem effortless; you know how hard you have worked and know that you deserve it. That business proposition you have is a sure thing, you have studied the market and know your product and believe that you can make it work. That big race coming up next month? You can already picture yourself at the finish line!

If you still doubt the benefits from building confidence then look no further than at some of the most successful people in the world. Leading scientists, entertainers, athletes, etc., have developed bold personalities and are all quite confident. They hold strong beliefs in their capacities, are assertive and quite tenacious. They will be the first to tell you their secret is persistence and to bounce back stronger after inevitable failures. You'll find that these individuals know it is critical to be their number one support and have unrequited doubt in themselves.

Of course, this doesn't mean that all you need to achieve your goals is a little faith in yourself. It must be known that confidence is not blind optimism, or put another way simply believing in yourself and expecting things to magically happen without a stitch of effort.

Though you have to believe that you will succeed, it is not recommended that you blindly charge into a situation without proper planning. You have to be prepared for any eventual mishaps by becoming resilient. However, too much confidence can turn into arrogance and that can be your downfall. If you think you can make it work by sheer will power, you are gravely mistaken. Confidence is the perfect balance between having the tenacity to seize new opportunities, an unwavering motivation and being meticulous enough to properly and skillfully navigate the task at hand.

Do not let the fact of not being an expert hold you back from achieving success. The saying, “Fake it until you make it” is actually quite powerful.

If you have ever seen the movie “Catch Me If You Can”, based on the life of high school dropout Frank W. Abagnale Jr.

In fact, without having any prior experience or formal education, Frank took it upon himself to teach sociology at Brigham Young University. He posed as the actual teacher even though he had no credentials whatsoever.

What was his secret? He simply read one chapter ahead of the class and then taught the lesson with confidence.

This showcases an excellent approach to one of the best ways to learn: Diligently focus on the new learning, task or skill at hand and pretend that you have to teach it to another person or group of people. This will force you to learn the ins and outs of said skill at a much faster pace.

However, I am *not* condoning that you commit fraud or deceive others in any capacity whatsoever. Quite the contrary. As you can see confidence is a powerful tool that can be used for good and self-improvement as well as for mischievous purposes.

Now, if you were given success on a silver platter or magically made confident, you may want to take a moment and think it through. Instant success will also certainly come with its own unexpected limitations due to the lack of exposure to valuable lessons along the way. Without these lessons the right mindset will not be formed and therefore your progress from that point forward will be handicapped.

Confidence will enable you to succeed at anything. It makes you dream bigger and pick up the necessary workload to turn those dreams into reality. It will also benefit other aspects of your life, you will be better able to express yourself among strangers and make new friends as people find confidence interesting and attractive. You will not miss any chances as it will make you less hesitant and you will be a better leader, making sure that your team's spirits stay high when things are not looking so good because you are certain of your abilities as well as theirs. That's right, being confident also helps you build other people up. If they are told they can achieve anything by someone who is sure of their success, they will not doubt themselves as much.

While you can manage to cruise through life by keeping a low profile, having low self-esteem and being too scared of failure to go after anything, that is no way to live. Everyone has dreams and aspirations and wants to be successful to become the best version of themselves. The difference between those who make it and those who don't is their belief in their success. It is up to you to build your confidence and build your self-esteem. You are the one who can grab life by the reins and make a conscious decision to take it to the next level.

This book is written to guide you through the journey to success but if you don't put in the necessary effort, it will remain just a book. You are the one with the power to take this life-changing information and use it to create a life full of confidence.

If you are ready to finally make a profound change and become someone who is practically invincible then keep on reading.

Carefully internalize the advice contained in these pages and then take massive action. With these simple, proven methods to manage your anxiety and shyness, you too can easily transform your personal and professional life.

Stop hesitating and get started right now!

Chapter 1: My Life with Shyness

Shyness is no new concept to me. It is something that I had to deal with for a good number of years. It always felt like these invisible restraints that kept me from experiencing life to the fullest. It messed up my personal and professional life in more ways than one. Because I was so shy, I didn't perform as well as I could at work. It also made forming new relationships more difficult than it should be. The thought of going out there and actually interacting with people made me dread my day.

Often, I would dream of being able to work from home. Other days, I wished I were invisible, which is decidedly less reasonable. Calling in sick to avoid going to work or claiming previous engagements to turn down an invitation were strategies I contemplated often before dragging myself out of the safety of my own home.

What I am trying to say is, being shy is all too familiar with me so I can relate to how you may be feeling. I understand your struggles and I want you to know that you can get over this. I was able to do it and I know for a fact that you can, too.

I don't want you to delude yourself into thinking that I woke up one day and my shyness was magically "cured", which is far from the truth. I made a lot of effort over the years to overcome my shyness. I built up my confidence and improved my social skills gradually over time. Looking back at how I was before, I feel that I have come a long way. The changes that I observed in myself are impressive and I want to share this experience in a way that would benefit you. I decided to organize the things that I have learned through trial and error over the years so you can avoid the pitfalls I experienced and you don't have to spend unnecessary time learning ineffective principles. Instead, you can use my experiences as a guide or a beacon of light to navigate smoothly through the application phase instead.

And speaking of the application phase, you have to do it. You have to actually apply what you will learn for any kind of growth to take place. You have to make the effort, there is no way around it. Believe me, the experience is worth it. You are worth it. At the end of the day, everything you learn and every effort you make will benefit you directly and you deserve to see the fruits of your labor. Your happiness is worth it.

Do you want to make a positive change? Well, it is a process and this book will see you through it.

Chapter 2: Understanding Shyness and Anxiety

Human beings like predictable patterns. They allow us to know what will happen next and stay in control. However, the thing about life is that it can get quite unpredictable. There are simply some aspects of life that we cannot change nor anticipate. We are often at the mercy of circumstances and while you can control how early you rise in order to make it to work early, you have no way to prevent an accident on the highway that will slow traffic down. The fact that we can't control all the variables in our lives makes us worry. We worry about what will happen and how to deal with it and all the ways it can affect our lives. This is natural, who doesn't like to be prepared to deal with a possible crisis? The thing is, if this worry gets out of control it can become a serious problem. And the name of that problem is anxiety.

Anxiety is one of the most easily recognizable disorders out there. You can often tell when you or someone has anxiety even without consulting a doctor. There are varying degrees of anxiety and while some forms of it are benign, others can turn into something very serious.

Shyness, however, is a bit different. Though you experience worry, it happens when you are in unfamiliar environments. You also tend to feel awkward in social settings *because* you worry about how you will be perceived.

What causes social anxiety is low self-esteem. You feel self-conscious about your appearance, personality, abilities and even your possessions. You feel less confident about those things and you worry about how you will be judged if they are set as standards.

Which one is it?

So, what are we dealing with here? Is it social anxiety disorder or shyness?

As mentioned before, anxiety has varying degrees of severity. It is sometimes tricky to know on which level you stand. Here are some telltale signs of anxiety:

- Quick heart rate
- Hyperventilation
- Excessive sweating
- Overthinking
- The urge to flee from a situation or hide from people
- A feeling of dread and apprehension

These are very common symptoms of anxiety.

It could be that your shyness is accompanied by anxiety, making it worse than what it is or that you are suffering from Social Anxiety Disorder.

SAD is a fear of being in social situations. People who suffer from it fear the prospect of being around people and more specifically, being judged by people.

The symptoms of SAD are the ones that are mentioned above. However, they are experienced more intensely.

Negative impacts of shyness and anxiety

Shy people tend to think that there is nothing wrong with being shy. You are not hurting anyone, are you? Well... you are. Your shyness might not be hurting anyone else, but it is hurting you. Sure, it might not be landing you in troublesome situations but the true cost is missing out on so many aspects of life. Being aware of that helps you find the courage you need to overcome it.

Here is how shyness is negatively impacting your life;

It can lead to loneliness

Because shy people are so reluctant to approach others, they are often lonely. They tend to keep to themselves and this means that they rarely get the chance to form meaningful and fulfilling relationships. Though some enjoy their alone-time, it is very easy to get bored and lonely without company.

Renders you unable to cope in random situations

This is caused by the anxiety you get from facing the unknown and new people fall under that category. A shy person would find it difficult to adjust to a sudden change and cope with unaccounted-for situations. This is because they find it hard to address others and ask for help or guidance.

Causes low self-esteem

When surrounded by others, a shy person can easily become self-conscious. They start over-thinking about their behavior and appearance and deem themselves not good enough. They also tend to read too much into others' behavior and think that they share the same negative thoughts that plague them. Oftentimes, this is wrong and the people around them are too focused on making a good impression themselves to judge.

Affects your confidence

When you have low self-esteem, you tend to think that everything about yourself is lacking. You second guess yourself and get discouraged from socializing. Every time you feel like you did something good, a voice in your head tells you that you didn't and proceeds to point out your mistakes or tell you what you should have done differently.

People get the wrong opinion about you

"When I first met you, I thought you were an arrogant snob." A lot of shy people hear these words from their friends. Maybe you did too. The truth is, it is very easy to form that kind of impression when meeting someone who seems unwilling to make the effort to be civil. Avoiding people, turning down invitations to hang out with them and staying quiet when you do join them make it seem like you think yourself above the company.

Despite the negative aspects mentioned above, shyness has its perks. Here are some positive traits that shy people are known for;

Shyness makes you a great listener

Because you don't speak that much, other people do most of the talking. Though this sometimes causes awkwardness and tense moments of silence when having a conversation, it can be very helpful when someone needs a good listener. You are good at listening without interruptions. It gives people the chance to unload their burdens, share their secrets and confide in you.

It makes you more sensitive to the emotional needs of others

The quietest people are often the most observant. Not having to focus on what you say enables you to better observe others, read their body language and subtle expressions. You are very perceptive when it comes to the emotions of others and can almost instantly recognize when something is wrong.

You are the best kind of friend

The fact that forming friendships doesn't come easily to you makes you cherish the friends you do have. You don't take the people in your life for granted and you are appreciative, loyal and caring towards your friends. Though shyness did play a role in you being a great friend, keep in mind that it is always thanks to who you are as a person. You are simply that great!

You think before you act (or speak)

Your self-consciousness and reluctance to express yourself, in general, makes you better able to think through your actions and words. It is very easy for people to say the wrong thing “spontaneously” but you usually don’t make that mistake.

You have a calming effect on people

The aforementioned reluctance to express yourself means that your reactions are always regulated. You always appear calm and unbothered. Though this might not be how you actually feel, you manage to keep yourself from showing signs of how nerved-racked you are. This is very helpful to the people around you in alarming situations as they tend to look for the calmest person in the room and use them as an anchor.

Chapter 3: Coping with Socially Triggered Anxiety and Managing Shyness

Now that you know the perks and cons of your shyness, it is imperative that you know how to manage the resulting anxiety. More specifically, the anxiety that you get as a shy person in social settings. The first thing to do when trying to do damage control is to identify the cause. In other words, finding out what causes your shyness will help you know which coping methods you should use.

Socially triggered anxiety, as its name indicates, happens when a shy person is in a social setting that requires them to interact with people. Though they all share the aspect of triggering anxiety, those settings vary depending on the occasion.

Getting out there

Simple things like eating out in public, going to the movie theater or even shopping can be terrifying to some people. The fact that they share a space with other people switches on their self-consciousness. They start wondering if they look weird or are behaving oddly and ask themselves questions like "Did I get sauce on my face?", "Am I blocking the view from the people sitting behind me?" "Would I bother the shop keeper if I ask him about the available sizes?"

Taking the lead:

Sometimes in life, we have to take initiative. This applies to both work and personal life. From time to time, we may have to take a leadership position at work and that means getting to know team members, assigning proper tasks to them and guiding them through their work. Each of these will require interacting closely with others, which at first, can seem to be a problem. Perhaps your career may require you to deliver speeches as a team leader to encourage your team or as any other type of public speaker. The activity itself can be terrifying to even the most confident of people out there.

Similarly, in personal life, we sometimes meet people who spark our interest. The fact that someone seems interesting enough for you to want to talk to already puts them on a pedestal and that can be very intimidating. It can be very difficult to take the first step and introduce yourself to a stranger who sparked your interest.

Thankfully there is an easy way to overcome this obstacle.

With a little preparation you can have a few ice breaker questions in your arsenal to get the conversation rolling:

- What is the scariest thing you've ever done for fun?
- If you were a type of jeans, what type would you be?
- If you had one extra hour of free time a day, how would you use it?

- Would you rather have more money or time?
- What failure have you learned the most from?
- Would you rather be known for your intelligence or good looks?
- Would you rather physically or mentally never age?
- What is your biggest turn off in a partner?
- What book has made the most profound and positive impact on your life?

Speaking up:

Standing up for yourself in moments of conflict is a scary prospect for shy people. Confrontations attract unwanted attention because people get offended when they are told their actions are bothersome. They become defensive and start raising their voices and sometimes even throw insults at you. Things can get ugly pretty fast when speaking up about what bothers you and that is why it can trigger your anxiety.

The scenarios mentioned above are just a few examples, there are countless other social situations that can make you anxious. Now, the question is why are some people perfectly fine in these situations while others are overwhelmed by their shyness? Better yet, what causes shyness in general?

1. Behavioral conditioning:

When we go through a negative experience, we fear repeating it. What we fear is not the experience itself but the negative outcome. Our brains love to establish patterns. When we go through a situation for the first time, we look for the outcome of the situation in question as a reference. Meaning that we believe that we will have the same result every time we go through the same situation in the future. Logically speaking, this is not right. However, you have to actively rewire your brain to understand that.

2. Individual thought process:

Your thoughts are responsible for many of your personality traits. They are also responsible for your feelings and behaviors. When you expect the worst, chances are, the worst will happen. On the other hand, going into a situation with a positive mindset, the outcome is very likely to be positive. This positive outlook on life will allow your confidence to grow as you firmly believe that good things will happen. As cliché as it may sound, "the glass is half full" is a powerful way to frame any situation and know that you have nothing to worry about.

3. Social conditioning:

This is relative to how you were raised. Your upbringing played a big role in how you have developed over the course of your life. Your shyness might have started to sprout in your early childhood as a result of the values and methods you were exposed to by your parents. Having parents who are controlling, aggressive or simply expect perfection at everything their child does can be a main reason behind a person's shyness. This is because of the constant criticism and reprimands. The child grows up believing they are not good enough regardless of what they do because they didn't receive the confidence-building encouragement as they progressed through life. If you are a parent yourself, heed this advice! Encourage and instill empowerment in your children so they know *anything* is achievable with the right mindset.

4. Biological reasons:

As odd as it seems, being shy can be a matter of genetics. You might have inherited your shyness from your ancestors. Even anxiety could be genetically passed from one generation to another. This doesn't mean that you are doomed to a life of seclusion, however. You can still work on your confidence and minimize the impact of shyness on your life.

No matter what causes your shyness and anxiety, you can still take control of your life and cancel out their impact on your behavior. It will take time and effort but it is possible and that is what you should be focusing on. It must be known that you need to be aware of the things that slow down your progress. It is very important you put an end to these behaviors the moment you become aware of them. Here are some examples:

A. **Being too self-conscious:**

When you are too self-conscious, you keep trying to find faults in yourself. The problem is, when you do that, you also start thinking that everyone else is aware of these faults which might not even exist in the first place. When you catch yourself doing that, stop. Remember that people are consumed with their own lives that they're less interested in keeping a tally of your flaws. Even if they are sitting there cataloging your imperfections for some unlikely reason, their opinion of you does not matter. The only one who matters is you. So, you beautiful human being, start thinking better of yourself and build up that confidence!

B. **Avoiding new situations:**

Getting out of your comfort zone is inevitable if you want to make progress. Yes, it can be scary; but the fact that you are reading this book and seeking to make a change tells me that you already have the courage it takes to face your fears. Change a few things in your routine, experience new situations and challenge yourself every day.

C. **Having negative thoughts:**

Negative thoughts lead to anxiety and low self-esteem and we do not want that. To counter negative thinking, you have to start seeing the bright side of things. Positive thoughts will help you appease your worries and by consequence, your shyness. Focus more on what is good and be grateful for it. List your strengths and think about them instead of your imperfections. It is good to be aware of reality as long as you focus on the positive aspects of life.

Chapter 4: Overcoming Shyness in the Workplace

Considering that you spend a good part of your time at home sleeping, it is safe to say that you spend more time with your coworkers than your family. Assuming that you have a nine to five job, of course. How you interact with those coworkers can impact your overall work experience greatly. Most workplaces encourage competition and sometimes, that can lead to a strained working environment. However, though you can't make your boss cancel the "Employee of The Month" program, you can still have a pleasant relationship with your colleagues. Whether you take that relationship to a friendship level or not is up to you, but you should at least make sure that you build a sense of camaraderie. When mutual respect is established and all people involved get along well, productivity will inevitably increase. This is a sure way for you to not only flourish as a confident individual but to become an integral part of the organization. Here are a few tips to help you with that:

Eye contact

One of the best ways to establish your presence is eye contact. It is a sign of confidence and belief in your capabilities. Eye contact is crucial during a conversation because it shows emotion or interest. Thankfully, it is a skill that can be developed and finely tuned. You never see someone who is sure of themselves casting their eyes down, do you? Good eye contact will even compensate for a quiet nature.

Just make sure you get it right. You don't want people to think you are staring or even glaring at them.

Here's an effective approach to making eye contact:

1. **Establish eye contact right away** - Before you even begin talking, make sure to establish eye contact. Avoid looking down or getting distracted by something before you begin to speak.

2. **Maintain eye contact** - Once you establish eye contact, maintain or hold it for **4 to 5 seconds**. After this time passes, you can start to let your eyes glance to either side and then back to establishing eye contact.

3. **The 50 / 70 rule** - You want to avoid staring at all costs! To appropriately maintain eye contact without staring, you should keep eye contact for about **50%** of the time while **speaking** and approximately of the time while **listening**. By implementing this rule, you will appear to genuinely display interest and confidence.

Greetings:

When people think you are ignoring them, they can easily label you as arrogant, impolite and rude. This is why greeting people when you first get into the office or when you cross paths in a hallway is a habit you should get into as soon as you start working. Sometimes, a nod, a wave or a smile by way of acknowledgment is all you need to do. This will give a good impression of you and your coworkers will see you in a positive and friendly light. Acknowledgement is also an easy way to show others you're appreciative and see them as humans.

Introductions

Walking up to a stranger and telling them a bunch of facts about yourself feels awkward, even to the best of us. But, do you know what would feel even more awkward? Having to do it after months of working with someone. You will have to introduce yourself sooner or later so you might as well save yourself the trouble and do it when you are freshly starting. It is much better to do it before anyone has gotten the chance to form any opinions about you, anyway.

Go ahead and break the ice with a firm handshake and simply say hello. The conversation doesn't have to be extensive. If you want to take a little further than introducing yourself, ask them a question about themselves. Talking about the weather is a meaningless topic and leads to nowhere.

Asking questions

You may think that asking questions will make you sound inexperienced, however there's nothing wrong with seeking advice. In fact, more often than not, people enjoy sharing their knowledge and appreciate when someone looks up to them. The ability to ask for advice can make you appear confident enough to rely on someone else's expertise for guidance. Regardless of how you view them, asking questions when you are not sure about something will save you a lot of work and embarrassment in the long run. You don't want to be that person who ruined a project because they were too proud to ask how things should be done. Besides, you would be surprised how many people seek an answer to the same question but are too shy to ask for help. Take initiative, muster up the courage and ask for help. Because in reality the answer to your question will also benefit other colleagues. Remember, "closed mouths don't get fed."

Don't shy away from challenges

Yes, the idea of getting into something that isn't a guaranteed win can be intimidating. And sometimes, you even have to compete with other people which makes it even more daunting. However, a good challenge can be a great way to prove yourself. You can showcase your skills and strengths. It can even present you with an opportunity to interact with your colleagues if it is done as part of a team. When there is a challenge at work, don't refuse it immediately. Believe in yourself and give it a shot. It can be very fun and you will probably end up benefiting from it even if you don't win.

Though the goal is to get along with the others, it is very important that you speak up in certain cases. Here are some examples:

1. **When you get an idea:**

   Ideas are the core of every profitable product out there. When you get an idea that you think might benefit the company, don't hesitate to share it with your boss. This shows that you are a valuable asset to the team and might even earn you a promotion. Besides, having your idea seriously considered and accepted as a potential project is a great confidence boost.

2. **When someone steals your idea for a project:**

   Though it sounds like something out of a drama series, this actually happens in reality. Some people have no problem with appropriating someone else's work. Never let it slide when someone takes credit for your work. Take it to your superiors and be very vocal about it.

3. **When you are being wrongfully accused:**

   This can have serious consequences. If your coworkers and superiors think that you are guilty of something you did not do, make sure to correct their beliefs. In cases like these, there might be more than your reputation at stake. You don't want to lose your job over something that you had no hand in. So, make sure to speak up and defend yourself.

4. **When you are being harassed:**

   Workplace harassment is more common than you might think. Some people believe that they can advance further by bullying others and you shouldn't accept that. Know our rights and report the ones harassing you to human resources or the proper authorities.

Chapter 5: Overcoming Anxiety in Social Settings

When in social settings unrelated to work, interactions are supposed to be more relaxed and casual. Don't be afraid to get more personal in those interactions. Try to form meaningful relationships or strengthen the ones you already have. At times it can get tricky, but it's usually well worth the effort.

Live in the moment:

Try to not think of any past situations that might have been embarrassing or uncomfortable. Those memories will make you relive the mortifying experiences and you will begin to think the same incident will occur again. When you feel yourself starting to panic because of past experiences, take a moment to calm yourself. Take a deep breath and remember that now and then are different times. If anything, you are more equipped to avoid those kinds of situations being that you have already gone through it.

"Perfection is the enemy of progress"

Originating and made famous by Winston Churchill, the phrase "Perfections is the enemy of progress" still rings true today. Let's face it, life is so unpredictable, and it is impossible to micromanage the perfect outcome in situations that are beyond our control. Of course, there are moments where everything is "perfect" but those are just part of the entire experience. It is always better to be pleasantly surprised than sorely disappointed, so don't expect perfection. Some would even argue that it is boring, anyway. Perfection leaves no room for growth or improvement.

Stay Oriented:

Becoming more aware of the people around you and devoting your full attention to the ongoing conversation is crucial to your journey in confidence building. However, never be afraid to admit that you are nervous because this shows that you are human and others will be better able to connect with you.

NOTE: Avoid using alcohol as a "quick fix" to your shyness, because this can easily lead to sloppiness and not being in complete control.

Explore:

Trying new things can help you adapt when you are thrown in unpredictable situations. Unplanned situations can arise at any moment when you are with other people. For example, someone may suggest participating in a game or you might be introduced to a friend's friend without any heads up. There's no way of preparing for these types of interactions other than fully embracing them when they may arise. So, you might as well gain some experience navigating these situations by diving into them head first. Through this exploration, seeking out situations or events that interest you is ideal so you can also have fun in the process.

10 Actionable Things You Can Do to Boost Self-Confidence

By now you understand that no one is born with complete self-confidence. It is cultivated and learned through experiences and a gradual trial and error. If you encounter someone who appears to have an endless supply of confidence and is constantly executing on their goals, it's because he or she has worked very hard to gradually build up their self-esteem and self-worth over a long period of time.

By challenging the world of business, and life in general your confidence skills will inevitably flourish and begin to come naturally to you.

The below tips can not only help boost your confidence, but also smoothly navigate situations of the unknown.

Actionable Tip!

1. **Visualize Your Ideal Self**

   Low self-confidence is the culprit that leads us to have a poor perception of ourselves. An effective way to raise your self-esteem is to visualize the person you want to become. Our thoughts are very powerful when it comes to helping achieve our goals. What does your ideal self-image look like or feel like? Mentally visualize being proud and happy of the person you will ultimately become.

2. **The Power of "No" and Personal Boundaries**

One of the most powerful words we can learn to say is, "no". As humans we tend to want to avoid hurting other people's feelings so reluctantly, we agree to do something we actually don't want to do. Set personal boundaries that teach people to respect your space and time. Learn to become more assertive and simply ask for what it is you want. It may be difficult at first, but practice saying no to things that do not help you achieve your goals. The first time you incorporate this habit, you will feel a wave of relief. This little word will allow you to gain more control over your life and in return your confidence will boost!

3. **Give Yourself Affirmations**

How you see yourself internally and externally is how you behave. This is a fact. Change the way you view your self-image and you have the power to create lasting change. The trick to implementing this process correctly is through affirmations.

Affirmations are powerful, uplifting and positive statements we say to ourselves. Because we often believe what we tell ourselves these statements are more effective when said out loud so you can hear it.

Biologically, our brains function in such a way that it will seek answers to questions without analyzing if the question is valid or not. With this in mind, affirmation can be rephrased as such:

A. "Why do I always have the knowledge to make smart decisions for myself?"

B. "Why I am so courageous all the time and willing to act and face my fears?"

C. "How do I always have everything that I need to make today a great day?"

D. "Why do I work well under pressure and always feel motivated?"

E. "How come my confidence is always rising?"

F. "How is it that I always let go of any negative feelings about myself or my life, and seem to accept all that is good?"

G. "Why do I have unlimited power?"

H. "How did I become such a powerful creator of the life I want?

I. "Why is it that every day I discover interesting and exciting new paths to pursue?"

J. "How did I become so focused on my goals and feel so passionate about my work?"

K. "Why do I always have everything I need to face any obstacles that come my way?"

L. "How come I always attract only the best of circumstances and I have the most positive people in my life?"

4. **Always question your inner critic**

We all have an inner critic, but we should never let it bring us down.

In fact, there are two different voices inside of all of us which guide us along in life. One that is loving and nurturing, and the other which is harsh and critical. The loving voice tends to lift us up, and contrarily the harsh voice weighs us down.

However, just as life is about balance, both of these voices play key roles. Our inner nurturing voice provides encouragement and self-compassion, while the inner critic teaches you where you went wrong and how to get things back on track.

Unfortunately for most people, the harsh inner critic can spin out of control and go overboard, slowly chipping away at your ego by shaming, nit-picking, scolding and faultfinding.

If you find yourself struggling with low self-confidence, there is a high chance that your inner critic has taken over and become overactive.

Cognitive behavioral therapy can help you to question and peel back the layers of your inner critic, and reveal evidence which supports or denies the things that your inner critic is telling you.

For instance, if you think that you are a complete failure, take a moment to ask yourself:

1. "Is there any evidence or rationale to support the thought that I am a failure?"

2. "Is there any evidence or rationale which does not support the thought that I am a failure?"

By questioning your inner critic, you will soon realize that you're often too hard on yourself and these negative thoughts do not make you who you are.

Lastly, no matter how big or small you should always find opportunities to congratulate, compliment and reward yourself. This can go a long way with helping build up your self-esteem and confidence.

5. 100 days of rejection challenge

The idea is simple. Every day you should seek to become rejected in something. By realizing that the worst that can happen is to hear the word "no", being rejected doesn't seem so bad after a while. The more you become desensitized to rejection, the faster your confidence will build.

As Jia Jiang stated, “The most effective way to overcome fear of rejection is to face it.” Jia decided to finally face his life-long fear of rejection by making wild requests throughout a 100 days of rejection challenge. The result? He actually had more people say *yes*, than say *no*!

Often people say “No” because they lack enough information to make a decision or because they feel they may be at risk if they do say “Yes”. Surprisingly, changing a “No” to a “Yes” is often as easy as asking “Why.”

This provides the person an opportunity to share what is making them uncomfortable with our request. Once you know why someone does not feel comfortable you can address these concerns instead of blindly assuming what the issue is. Or, even worse, giving up altogether when you get rejected.

Understand the “Why” and you’ll be more prepared to face rejection with confidence. Who knows, you might even just hear that golden “Yes” when you least expect it.

6. **Set yourself up to win**

Too many people get discouraged about their abilities because they set goals for themselves that are too difficult to achieve in their first attempt. Start by setting small goals that you can win easily.

Once you have built up a stream of successes that make you feel good about yourself, you can then move on to harder goals. Make sure that you also keep a list of all your achievements, both large and small, to remind yourself of the times that you have done well.

Instead of focusing only on "to-do" lists, I like to spend time reflecting on "did-it" lists. Reflecting on the major milestones, projects and goals you've achieved is a great way to reinforce confidence in your skills.

Actionable Tip!

Create S.M.A.R.T. Goals - There's a difference between "I want to be a rich" and "I want to make $75,000 a month for the next twenty years by developing a new software product".

Specific, Measurable, Attainable, Relevant, Timely

Set **Specific Goals** - What exactly do you want to achieve? The more specific your description is, the higher probability you'll get exactly that.

Set **Measurable Goals** - Identify exactly what it is you will feel, see and hear when you reach your goal. This means breaking down your goal into measurable pieces.

Set **Attainable Goals** - Investigate whether your goal is

actually acceptable to you. Weigh out the time, effort and other costs your goal will require against the profits and any other obligations and priorities you currently have.

Set **Relevant Goals** - Is obtaining your goal actually relevant to you? Do you really want to become famous, run an international company, have four children and a busy career? Make the decision to whether you have the personality for it, or your team has the bandwidth.

Set **Timely Goals** - Time is one of the only things we cannot make more of. Make a plan for everything you do. Deadlines will force you to action and execute your goals in a timely manner. Remember to keep the timeline realistic and flexible so you do not set yourself up for failure.

By setting S.M.A.R.T. goals you can create "mini wins" and build up your confidence slowly.

7. Help someone else

Helping someone else can be one of the most rewarding feelings you ever get.

This reminds us to feel grateful for what we have. It also feels amazing when you are able to make a significant difference for someone else. The key is to avoid focusing on your own perceived weaknesses and shift your energy to more meaningful activities such as assisting or teach someone a new skill or even volunteering. The sheer joy derived from this experience alone will give you an amazing boost of natural self-confidence.

8. **Do one thing that scares you every day**

As mentioned previously, the best way to overcome any fear is to face it directly head-on. By doing something that scares you every day and gaining confidence from every experience, you will see your self-confidence skyrocket. So, step out of your comfort zone, do that crazy yet reasonable thing and face your fears!

9. **Give yourself some TLC**

As you know, how you view yourself is directly correlated to your level of self-confidence. If you fully love who you are, it will show in the way you treat your physical body as well. The golden trifecta to unlocking self-confidence comes from a blend of good physical health, emotional health and social health.

Let's explore this a little further.

1. **Increase in Physical Activities**

Think about this for a moment ... Not only does exercising regularly improve physical strength and endurance, but in fact exercise is also paramount to boosting your inner strength and confidence as well. By making a commitment to yourself to exercise on a regular basis, and prioritizing fitness, you will become more confident.

On the other hand, a lack of physical fitness can lead to extremely low energy levels which will reflect in your self-esteem, how you view the world and the way you carry yourself.

You don't have to be a gym rat or a competitive athlete to experience the benefits from an increase in physical activity.

By incorporating a simple fitness routine, you will be surprised at how much more confident you will be and have a performance in all aspects of your life.

2. **Improve Your Sleeping Habits**

In addition to becoming more physically active, make sure you are also getting an adequate amount of sleep. Without sufficient sleep we can easily become overwhelmed by the hustle we experience in everyday life. Inadequate sleep will often lead to augmented feelings of stress, lack motivation and making us highly sensitive.

3. **Better Eating Habits**

   When our energy levels decrease, we often seek out unhealthy snacks full of sugar to give us that jolt of energy, but unfortunately this boost only lasts a short while and ends up making us feel even worse in the long run. You don't have to go extreme and follow the latest organic keto fasting all vegetable and water diet. But there is a strong correlation to what we put in our bodies for fuel and how we operate. Think about how an engine operates with special fuel. With lower quality fuel or even lack of maintenance, the engine begins to gradually wear down and ultimately stops functioning. Similarly, the same thing happens with our bodies! Incorporate better eating habits by consuming less sugar and substituting it with some whole foods such as vegetables.

10. A Mentality of Equality

Repeat this out loud:

I AM ENOUGH. I, AM ENOUGH. I, AM, ENOUGH!

Avoid having the perception that you are not enough by comparing yourself to others. Each person has a unique life and their own struggles. That is not you.

Those with low self-confidence will see those around them as superior or more deserving than themselves. Instead of falling victim to this perception, view yourself as an equal to everyone.

I cannot stress enough that these people are no more deserving or better than you. Make a conscious decision to mentally shift the perception of yourself by knowing you are an equal.

Heed my warning: This shift in mentality has been shown to make a dramatic improvement in one's self-confidence.

Conclusion

Thank you very much for taking the time to read this book! Now that you have successfully made your way through it, you have the theoretical knowledge you will need to boost your confidence and take massive action.

We covered many topics and no doubt there is a lot of information to digest. The best approach going forward is not to feel overwhelmed by the amount of options to boost your self-confidence, but instead to pick two or three tips and put them into action immediately!

Reading and taking action will be the difference between you understanding theoretically how to improve your self-worth and actually seeing massive results. Take it slow and gradually see what works best for you.

Perseverance and grit will pave the path to your ultimate progress. Do not let failures veer you of course, but use them as stepping stones to your success as you begin to learn from each experience. This book was written with the firm belief that you too can achieve greatness and we completely believe in your ability to reach your goals. Now get up and start working on building that confidence. The world is full of incredible opportunities and possibilities and with your new-found confidence they are ripe for the taking!

Book 6.

How to Talk to Anyone

A Guide to Mastering Your Social Skills and Small Talk, Develop Charisma, How to Win Friends, Influence People with 53 Easy Conversation Topics You Can Use to Effortlessly Speak to Anyone

INTRODUCTION

As you go through your everyday life, interacting with people can hardly be avoided. Humans are social creatures and it is virtually impossible to go to a social event without speaking to anyone at some point. In fact, even brief interactions such as paying for your purchase at a store requires a minimum amount of talking to people. You might not like it, you might be an introvert, suffer from social anxiety or are just not that talkative by nature, but there isn't much you can do once you are addressed by someone or need to address someone yourself. True, the internet and various mobile apps have made it possible to minimize the amount of interaction when it comes to online shopping or ordering food but think about situations where it simply is not possible. A visit to the doctor's office, for instance. Can you imagine staying quiet throughout the entire examination? It's simply not possible. Your doctor will inevitably ask you questions and you will need to provide answers that will help diagnose you. Another example is a job interview. The person interviewing you will be able to get a lot of information just from talking to you. If your skills were all that mattered, they would have hired you just from looking at your resume and while you can work from home, that simply is not an option for some people. In situations like these, having the ability to talk to anyone is necessary.

It is true that some people find it easier to approach strangers than others. It is even effortless to them. They can even talk to someone they just met and be perfectly at ease. However, this is unfortunately not the case for a lot of people. If you are one of them, don't worry. The ability to talk to anyone can be learned and perfected through practice. This ability will come in handy when trying to make friends, building business relations or dissipating an awkward silence.

Being able to start a conversation and keep the interest of who you are talking to is not as hard as it seems once you have the basic knowledge you need to approach people.

People have used speech as a way to communicate since the very beginning. Through talking to others, humans have expressed their feelings, transferred knowledge, solved problems and requested help. People who have conversational skills are, to this day, assigned important work that requires wisdom and intelligence. Ambassadors, marketers, teachers and a lot of other professions that require persuasion skills, negotiation skills, and refined social skills. Can you imagine the number of wars that were avoided thanks to proper communication between countries? Ambassadors are usually people who know what to say and how to word it, often smoothing the process for the people in charge. They can use their words to diffuse a delicate situation and maintain peace. It is true that they are aware in both countries' political stance but they rely more on their ability to wield words than factual knowledge in their interactions.

While you might not aspire to represent your country, honing your communication skills will help you improve many aspects of your life.

For once, you will get into social situations feeling more confident as you would have a better ability to interact with people. You will be able to navigate school life and work more efficiently as you will know how to deal with different people, whether they are your fellow students, teachers or administrative staff. You will also be better able to maintain your personal relationships and form new ones. Making friends will be much easier and will go as the stress-free process that it is supposed to be.

If you still cannot see the benefits of learning how to talk to people properly, think of that one successful friend you have. They are doing great at their work, they are great in gatherings, talking to strangers is a piece of cake and you can even introduce them to your parents with the guarantee that they will be charmed. That friend is not like that because they are likable by nature or because they can secretly cast spells on others to gain their affection. They have merely developed their communication abilities and have become so good at using them now that they make talking to people look easy. And those who are often referred to as silver-tongued are usually just good at using the right words on the right person.

When you get the hang of making day to day conversation and move on to knowing how to go about special situations by understanding social cues and reading the mood, your life will be much easier. You see, in most cases, it is just a matter of speaking with poise and telling people what they want to hear. Sometimes, surprisingly you do not have to make much of an effort at all. Simply stay clear of problematic or polarizing topics such as politics or religion and make sure you don't offend anyone. If you're really lucky, you might find yourself conversing with someone who knows how to keep the conversation going and the effort will be split between the two of you to make it work.

Now, the way we are addressing it, makes conversations sounds like a very daunting topic, doesn't it? In reality, it actually isn't that bad and you may end up enjoying it. Of course, there will be occasions in which you will have to make tedious small talk and speak about something that doesn't interest you. But you will also meet interesting people with whom you will enjoy talking with. There will be instances where you discover shared interests between you and your conversation partner and you might look back to that particular conversation one day feeling grateful that you made the effort to speak with who would later become a dear friend.

Now, for all of that to happen you have to be willing to physically get out there and talk to people. This is something that is entirely up to you. You alone hold the power to take action and make the decision of learning this skill. This book is merely but a tool that you can rely on in your journey. It will make some concepts clearer and organize the process for you.

If you are ready to make that effort to improve your conversational skills and learn how to talk to anyone, keep reading. Learning this skill will open doors for you that you never even knew existed.

Chapter 1: Communication and Development

Of all living beings, humans have the advantage of using words to communicate. This particular asset reflects a person's intelligence and social skills when interacting with others. Language plays a huge role in shaping individuals as well as communities. It influences the culture, beliefs, and social norms. In individuals, language not only plays the role of a medium to transfer knowledge and information, but it also intervenes in the emotional development of the individual. People learn how to express feelings and thoughts at a young age through interacting with others through language and non-verbal communication. The latter plays a big role in expressing feelings and is usually in the form of facial expressions, body language, and eye contact. However, these indicators can sometimes be misinterpreted and emotions are ideally expressed through words. Furthermore, verbal communication and more specifically conversations, help the development of a person's emotional intelligence. Through conversations, people develop a sense of empathy and are better able to hone their social skills such as recognizing social cues and using language that fits the context. Conversations also allow people to form and maintain meaningful relationships.

Three pillars of communication

To understand communication, you have to be aware of its three pillars.

Non-verbal communication

Though it is easy for a person to bend words to their will and use them to lie and manipulate, non-verbal signs are trickier. Our body language betrays a lot about us that is left unsaid. When we were young, our parents would instantly know that something wasn't quite right by our reluctance to make eye contact. You might even have seen it in the movies; instances where detectives pay close attention to a suspect's body language and analyze their movements to determine whether or not they are telling the truth. In fact, elbowing someone or winking at them can easily communicate that you want them to do something in a subtle way. Pay close attention to non-verbal signs when having a conversation and learn to interpret them correctly in order to improve your skills as a conversationalist.

Communication skills

These skills reflect your prowess as a conversationalist. This includes your ability to use the right words to express yourself, the capacity to get the desired response from your conversation partners and how good you are at keeping the conversation going.

Assertiveness

Being assertive not only shows how confident you are but it also allows you to stay true to yourself. This doesn't mean that you have to dominate the conversation without a care for the feelings and comfort of others, however. You can still be honest about your views and fearlessly express your opinions without disrespecting other people.

Becoming a good conversationalist takes a lot of practice. You may say the wrong things sometimes or fail to catch certain indicators but it is these mistakes that help you make progress. Through your journey to success, you may face some obstacles and fear is one of them.

Fear

It is one of the biggest obstacles that you would have to overcome in order to become a better conversationalist. It can be the fear of interacting with others in general or something more specific. For instance, you might be afraid of judgment, embarrassment, conflict, causing offense or any sort of negative outcome that may result from a conversation. Usually, fear stems from past experiences that went wrong, your mind leads you to believe that you will be facing the same outcome and that makes you afraid of repeating the experience. The truth is, you may never overcome your fear completely but you can decrease its intensity so that you will be better able to manage it.

Rate your fear

In order to control your fear, it is important that you understand its extent. Rating your fear will enable you to determine what it will take to face it. It may help if you make a scale of things that scare you and use them to classify your fear of conversing with others. For example, is it worse or better than your fear of the dark? Of heights? Of spiders? Those are just examples, you know your own fears best. Asking yourself the following questions will also help you rate the intensity of your fear.

- What causes you to be afraid of speaking with others?

- When did this fear develop?
- What caused the development of this fear?
- What was the context? i.e. the people involved, the settings, the sounds, etc.
- When was the last time you experienced a similar feeling to that fear?
- Who was with you?
- How did you react to it?
- How did it go at the end?

After asking yourself these questions, rate your fear on a scale of 0 to 10. Try to also rate your level of coping if you face that fear again.

Rating your fear helps you by establishing a point of reference that you can use as a starting point. You will be better able to face your fear when you know where you stand.

Dwell on it

Facing your fear is all about getting out of your comfort zone and into the situation that scares you. The more you do it, the better you get at managing your fear. What happens is, the repeated exposure to what scares you will force you to come to terms with the fact that it isn't all that scary, in reality. Sometimes, though, you don't get many chances to put yourself in the kind of situation that sparks your fear and, in that case ... dwelling on it is a good alternative. The idea is to imagine yourself in the situation in question and to visualize how you would deal with your fear in that context. In this virtual scenario, you have the advantage of using different approaches and seeing the situation from different angles. This will not only prepare you to face your fears in real life, but it will also redirect your thoughts into viewing an intimidating situation differently.

Face it

After rating your fear and thinking through how you can face it, the next step is to face it. Get out there and step into a situation that you find frightening. Keep in mind that you already know how to handle this, you are just putting that knowledge to test. Get into social settings and interact with strangers. You can start slowly by speaking to one person at a time. After that, you can speak to different people on the same occasion. Then, you can start making conversations with groups of people

Chapter 2: Basic Guide to Good Conversations: What to Do & Not Do

Though conversations can be very flexible and tend to vary depending on the subject and the people involved, there are some guidelines to respect when having one. Rules, etiquette or good practices; whatever you choose to call them, these guidelines will help you become a great conversationalist and will allow you better control of the conversation;

You

The following guidelines concern you. They tell you what your behavior and attitude should be like when holding a conversation;

Don't steal all the spotlight

While it is alright to be the center of attention among people you know, it tends to be different when conversing with strangers. Bragging about your accomplishments and singing your own merits will make you seem arrogant and narcissistic. Sometimes, you do it with the intention to show that you are someone worth knowing but people might get the wrong idea. Remember that when you are talking to new people, you have a clean slate and the first impression you want them to have of you is a positive one.

It's not all about you

Just like you, other people are concerned about the impression that they will be making in a party of strangers. This means that they will probably not notice the missing button on your cuffs nor will they see the pimple you found on your chin when you woke up. They are too worried about themselves to focus their attention on you. If they do notice, make the best of the situation by joking about it. They must have had their fair share of clumsiness in other events so they will relate. Besides, it is a good chance to strike a lighthearted conversation.

Empathy is everything:

Having empathy is a sign of emotional intelligence and is always a good asset to have when holding a conversation. People appreciate those who have the ability to see things from their perspective and make an effort to understand their struggles. Listen and try to put yourself in the other person's shoes. When you disagree about something, do it with class. Even if you find yourself talking to someone who cannot see past their own nose, be the mature one. Always part with others with impeccable manners and flawless behavior.

Encourage them to talk about themselves:

The most considerate people are the most appreciated. We already established that you shouldn't monopolize the attention when you are holding a conversation, what you should do instead is encourage others to talk about themselves. Asking them about their interests and showing that you genuinely want to know more about them makes you someone they enjoy to talk with. Furthermore, try to create opportunities for others to have a part in the conversation. People like to feel included and if you make an effort to speak about common interests, it will keep the conversation going.

Elevate your energy:

Speaking with good cheer and enthusiasm breathes life into a conversation. We all had those dull talks with people who speak in a monotone voice and half-lidded eyes and it's never fun. Show interest when speaking with your conversation partner and express your views confidently. The positive energy you emit will be contagious and the conversation will be a lot more interesting.

Be inquisitive:

This means to ask questions. Act like an empty vessel that gets gradually filled with all the information you receive. Ask people about themselves, their interests, their work, their family. If you happen to be speaking with a specialist in a field other than your own, ask them about aspects of their profession that intrigues you. This not only shows interest in others, but it also helps maintain a meaningful conversation.

Conversation:

Conversations are unpredictable. You never know what turn a conversation will take or how it will end. You sometimes manage to leave a conversation with an altered view or having learned something new. That is what makes conversations so interesting. The fact that you can't know for sure how they will be progressing. That doesn't mean that you should unleash your thoughts without some sort of control when you are having a conversation. There are some rules that all parties should respect when having a conversation. Conversing with people should stay comfortable and proper. No one should feel insulted or uneasy and everyone's opinion must be respected. Here are a few pointers to help you along;

Keep the conversation flexible:

This was said before, conversations are unpredictable. A conversation can take an unexpected turn, it can shift into a different topic, it can be interrupted or simply die down. Your job is to keep up with the pace of the said conversation. If it stops, start another conversation about a different subject. The better your ability to adapt to the dynamics of the conversation, the better conversationalist you are.

Don't avoid small talk:

Small talk is often viewed as a meaningless way to start a conversation, a waste of time, basically. However, it is more important than you might think. You can rely on small talk to make a good first impression and it helps you get a feel of your conversation partner's personality. You can say it is a way to test the waters when talking to a new person. It also helps you set the pace for what comes next and allows you to smoothly transition into a deeper discussion.

Be on the lookout for sensitive topics:

When speaking to someone for the first time, try to stay away from sensitive topics. This means that you should avoid talking about anything that can potentially cause conflict in case of a difference in opinions. Politics, religion, death and even sports are things that people are very passionate about and that can affect their objectivity. Keep these subjects for when you are better acquainted with the person you are conversing with.

Observant:

Observing the people you are speaking with can help you determine how the conversation is going. Pay attention to their expressions, body language and any subtle movements they can make. Their behavior and reactions to what is being said should guide your own response.

Check the non-verbal signs:

Eye contact, stance, expressions, and body language can clue you in on how the conversation is progressing. If a person keeps checking the time when speaking to you, chances are they are not interested in the conversation. If they yawn or space out, they are probably bored. If they frown and cross their arms, you might have just said something problematic or offensive. Learn to read these subtle hints so that you can redirect the conversation to something more interesting or less risqué.

Chapter 3: The Best 53: Topics to Make Easy and Interesting Conversations

A good conversation is structured so that it begins with an Opener/Starter which represents the introduction of the conversation. Then, it transitions into Details and Filler, this part is the body of the conversation and it can include multiple topics. Finally, it ends with and Ender/Exit which is when the parties involved put an end to the conversation before parting ways.

Opener / Starter:

This may be the hardest part of holding a conversation. It is difficult because people don't usually know where to start and feel nervous. It is, however, the most important part because it sets the tone of the conversation and allows you to make a first impression. Basic conversation etiquette dictates that you start by introducing yourself before saying anything else. Here are a few examples;

Excellent starters / Openers:

Great conversation openers should not sound cliché. Stay away from discussing the weather, asking where they come from and whether they come here often. Instead, ask them about anything interesting that may have happened to them during the week or strike a conversation about the event you are currently at. Make use of your surroundings to start a conversation like the venue where the event is held or any influential people who might be present. Here are some suggestions that might be useful to you:

1. Hello, I'm _____. How are you?

2. Are you acquainted with the host?

3. This is quite a _____ event. Have you been to anything similar before?

4. What brings you here?

5. This is a _____ place. I remember going to _____ with a similar vibe. Where are you from?

6. The crostinis are _____! Don't you think? Is there anything you would recommend?

7. What do you do for a living?

8. Did you know _____ will be attending this conference as well?

Details / Conversation Fillers:

This is where you are supposed to take the conversation to a deeper level. You can speak about subjects with more substance and you can even ask personal questions if you think it would appropriate. Try to transition to this phase from the starters you used at the beginning. Here are some examples that you can follow up with assuming you had started the conversation with small talk about the venue or the event that is being held:

This is a _____ place. I remember going to _____ with a similar vibe. Where are you from?

8. Oh, that is not very far/close from here. I live at _____. I am currently staying at _____. Are you staying at a hotel nearby?

9. Do you have any relatives there?

10. Did you go to university there as well?

11. What did you major in?

12. Where do you work?

13. What does your work entail?

Are you acquainted with the host?

14. You do? Where did you meet him/her?

15. You don't? I happen to know him/her. We met at _____. We have kept in touch. He/she is very good at his/her job. If you are ever in need of a good host, he/she would be a good candidate. Do you know other hosts with as much experience?

16. Events business has become very popular nowadays, hasn't it? I see a lot of pictures on social media and they are very beautiful.

17. Do you happen to know anyone in the same line of work?

18. Who would you recommend? Do you have their contact information?

19. One time, I heard/saw/experienced this thing _____ with an event organizer. It is basically _____. There was _____ and _____. Did you experience anything like that? What was it and How did it go?

This is quite a _____ event. Have you been to anything similar before?

20. What was the most memorable thing about that event?

21. I think that this sort of event is_____. I was once told that _____. Unbelievable, right? What do you think about that?

22. Are you enjoying this event?

23. Do you think this event can be improved? How would you go about it?

24. There was this event I went to once and a few unexpected things happened. ______. What do you think about that?

What brings you here?

25. Do you know many people here?

26. I know the _____. We are ______. Do you know who that is?

The crostinis are _____! Don't you think? Is there anything you would recommend?

27. I once had to go through the unpleasant experience of eating _____. I had been at ______, it was held for the occasion of _____. Not much after I had arrived at ________. Did you ever eat something that you disliked that much?

28. I am a foodie, always have been. I really enjoy watching cooking videos on this YouTube channel called _____. Do you also enjoy cooking shows and the like?

29. Whenever I travel, I make sure to try the cuisine that the area is known for. I went to _____ and the local food was amazing. Have you ever been there before? Have you ever had the ______? What did you think of it?

30. Do you love traveling, also?

31. Where have you visited in the past?

A. Anything notable happen while you were there?
B. Did you find the food enjoyable?
C. Any excellent tourist spots?
D. I'm planning to visit ______, too soon. What place do you recommend?
E. Where's the best place to stay or visit?

32. I just remembered something weird. I once went to a deli / restaurant in _____ and their specialty was ______. It's very peculiar, isn't it? What's the weirdest food you have ever been served?

What do you do for a living?

33. Really? That sounds like an interesting job. What do you usually do as a/an _____?

34. What is your company called? In which business does it operate?

35. Well, I work as a/an _____ for a _____ company. My job is to ______ and ______. Is that similar to what you do at work?

36. How long have you had that job? What do you enjoy about it?

37. Well, I have had my current job for _____, now. I previously worked at _____ as a/an_____. I quit that job after a while because_____. I enjoy the _____ aspect of my present job. How about you? What do you think are the attractions of a job?

38. If you had to choose between pay and culture which would you go for? Why is that?

39. Yes, I can't argue with that. I once worked with someone who ______. He/she ______, and after a while ______. What do you think about situations like that?

40. What is the most unforgettable thing that happened to you at work?

As shown above, a conversation can take various directions even if it is started by the same opener. It is up to you and what you would like to know about the person you are speaking with. As long as you are genuinely interested in them and are willing to share a bit about yourself in return, you can ask them any questions that can further the discussion. The best way to do that is to volunteer a fact about yourself and then ask them about the same thing: **"I am_____. What about you?"**

The point is to pass the staff to your partner so that they can do their part in keeping the conversation flowing. Remember not to phrase your question in a way that would elicit a yes or no answer as that might bring the conversation to an end.

Conversation exit:

The conversation exit, like the Starter, is a bit tricky. Mainly because you have to end the conversation at a time where it has become interesting and after your partner has taken an interest in you. You have to end the conversation gracefully and maintain the good impression your partner has formed about you.

The main factor to consider is timing. You have to be aware of the time and make sure that you also have enough time to bid your party goodbye. You can wait until the clock strikes a certain hour and say that you have another engagement or even ask a friend to come to remind you that it is time for you to leave. Make sure the people you were speaking with know that you enjoyed speaking to them and that you enjoyed getting to know them. Tell them that you hope there will be a chance for you to converse with them again soon and exchange business cards or contact information before leaving.

The Powerful Art of small talk:

We have already established the importance of small talk. It allows you to set the pace of the conversation and then to transition into deeper subjects. It also allows you to make a good impression which will help you control the flow of the conversation later on. However, you have to be confident and know how to go about it correctly to get the desired results. You can make small talk sound very interesting if you have the proper set of skills to do so. It is tricky in a way that any miscalculated words may lead to awkward results but even that can be remedied by a skilled conversationalist. Here are a few examples of topics that are safe for small talk in any given context;

41. All about the weather

This is by far the most common topic for small talk and for good reason. People have discussed the weather to break the ice for hundreds of years and though it may be cliché, it is unlikely to cause you any problems. The interesting thing about the weather is that it varies from one day to another and you can come up with a lot of topics revolving around it.

A. Though the roads are a bit hard to navigate in this rain, I think it is much better than the scorching heat of the summer. The ideal would be to have cold weather without all the rain, don't you think?

B. This is a great day, isn't it? The weather is just perfect. I always enjoyed the spring. Sunny and not too hot nor too cold. Do you also enjoy this type of weather?

42. People

There are countless topics that can be inspired by your surroundings. People are a good subject to start with when you are starting a conversation. People are interesting because every single person is unique and they all have different looks and personalities. So, when you are thinking of a good starter topic, look around you at the people who are present. Be kind when you speak about others however, there is a very thin line between harmless gossip and backbiting.

A. I don't think I have ever seen so many kids running around at this kind of event before. Do you have any children?

B. If you look over there, you can see Mrs. _____. She owns a shoe store where you can find the most comfortable high heels and the sturdiest boots. Whenever I go there, I end up buying two pairs of shoes instead of one. Have you ever been to her store? Do you know any other nice stores around? Do you live nearby?

43. Sceneries

Another potential topic that you can come up with from watching your surroundings is sceneries. Especially if the event is held at an outside venue. Pick an interesting view and use it to make small talk and then make a smooth transition into other topics.

A. The lake is beautiful, isn't it? I love how the sunshine reflects off its surface. I even saw ducklings swimming around earlier. In winter a thin layer of ice covers the surface but it sadly isn't thick enough for skating. I'm sorry, if you are from around here you probably already know all of this, right? Oh, you are not? Where are you from? Are you staying at the ______ inn?

B. Do you see those trees on the other side of the estate? They are _____ trees. They were planted by the very first owners of the estate. They still bear fruit to this day. Have you ever seen them in spring when the flowers are in full bloom? Do you live nearby?

C. I love that old shed over there. When I was a kid, we used to play hide and seek around here and we used to fight over who gets to use it as a hiding place. Did you have a favorite hiding area when you were a child? Do you have any children? Are they fond of the game as well?

44. Events & Seasons

If there are any particularities about the time of the year, it may be worth talking about. Holidays and special occasions or any other special event is a good topic to broach when trying to start a conversation.

A. It's gotten quite cold, I hope we will have a white Christmas. Is this your first Christmas here?

B. The children are getting very excited about Easter. Do you also let the kids participate in making Easter eggs in your household?

45. Personal experiences

This one can be harder to handle. Asking personal questions can seem invasive and nosey. Try to observe your partner and get a read on their character and then decide if speaking about personal matters is a good idea or not.

A. You seem lost in your thoughts. Is there anything bothering you?

B. You look like someone worth knowing. Would you care to tell me more about yourself?

46. Sports & Games

While sports can be the subject of an entire conversation on their own, they can also be used as conversation starters. No matter what time of the year it is, the chances are there is a sports event going on. Perhaps it's the football season or the NBA playoffs, your favorite Hockey team may be playing next week or the Olympics are being held.

"The World Cup is coming to an end, I wonder who will win? It's a pity we didn't make it to the finals, which team are you cheering for?"

47. Common interests

Having a common friend or having gone to the same university can give you the perfect opportunity to start a conversation. It gives you and your partner a sense of camaraderie and it can instantly put you at ease.

A. I see you are wearing a _____ University sweater. I went there as well. What was your major?

B. Have you known Mason for long? He's my brother but I think this is the first time we've seen each other.

48. Music

There are not many people out there who dislike music. Regardless of the genre, music is something that has been a popular art for a long time. It is also very diverse so you can find a lot of topics revolving around it. If there is music playing at the event you are attending, use it as an asset and start up a conversation around the band or orchestra.

"I have never heard music from this band before but I really love what they are currently playing! Do you, by any chance, know the title of this song? Are you a fan? Do you often listen to this genre of music?"

49. Current events

You can get informed on current events through the news, the papers, and even social media. What is happening in the world is something that you can speak about because chances are, your partner has heard of it as well. However, make sure your opinions don't sound offensive to the other party who might see things from a different perspective and if that is the case, be patient and empathetic.

A. I cannot believe what is happening with the rainforest. For a place that produces 20% of the Oxygen in the world to burn like that is cause for worry. Do you think the situation can still be salvaged?

B. There have been a lot of protests in France since the new president made the new changes. It seems like the situation keeps escalating. What do you think about what is happening there?

50. Work

Work is one of the safest topics to use as a conversation starter. It is not problematic in any way and is neutral in a way that you describe routines and give information about what you do instead of expressing opinions. Typically, you discuss the nature of your work and the type of company you work for. You can also discuss culture and any particular policies you think are worth mentioning. (Refer to items 31-38)

51. Hobbies and Crafts

This is a very interesting topic and can be used as a starter in any context as well. If you are attending an event where artists or crafts enthusiasts may be in attendance, use it to strike up a conversation. It's nice to know something about the craft or hobby in question, but if you don't it can be a great opportunity to learn more about it while starting a conversation. Just show genuine interest and the other party will take care of the rest as they tell you more about the subject.

"Pottery has always seemed like a very relaxing and fulfilling craft. I have always wanted to try it but I haven't found a pottery school near my place where I can learn it. Can you tell me about the process? Are there different types of clay that you can use?"

52. World issues

This can be a sensitive subject to speak of. You have to be empathetic, respectful and tactful when speaking about world issues with others especially since opinions can vary depending on the subject. You have to be familiar enough with the subject, make sure you don't have any experiential lack or disadvantage and be mindful of all parties in case the topic involves social diversity relating to race, ethnicity, religion, political views, etc. Be open to other people's views on the subject and try to forget any biases you may have. There are always different sides to the same story and by speaking to other people, you get to see things from different points of view. If you are not knowledgeable enough on something, ask and show that you are willing to learn. Letting others educate you on a matter that you are ignorant about is better than claiming that you know everything and embarrassing yourself.

53. Anything else of interest

Everything that surrounds you can be made into a topic of conversation. You can speak and ask questions about anything.

Remember that there is a story to everything and everyone. The old lady that feeds the doves at the park, the ancient building on the outskirts of town and the young man who is always trying to recruit you for the local animal shelter. You can hear their stories and later tell them yourself to other people. All you need is an interest in those things and the ability to make them into an interesting topic to talk about.

Chapter 4: Conversation Put into Practice

The best way to improve at anything is to practice, no secret there. You have learned from the previous chapters how to manage your fear, read people's body language and use small talk to improve your conversation skills. So, you already know all you need to know in theory. The next step is to put that knowledge into practice. Get into social settings and start having conversations. Here are more tips to help you in your endeavor

Avoid one-word answer questions:

Curt answers are always awkward. They can make you sound aloof and uninterested and will bring the conversation to a stop. This is the case for both parties. Try to avoid answering questions with yes or no and if your partner does it, don't get discouraged and think of ways to keep the conversation going. Asking a question of your own after giving your answer is a good way to maintain the flow of the discussion.

Alternatively, another approach is to ask questions that are open-ended.

Open-ended questions initiate a conversation because they cannot be answered with a simple one-word answer. Here are some examples of open-ended questions:

- “Where would you like to be in five years from now?”
- “What are the top priorities for your business this year?”
- “What do you want to accomplish this year?”
- “What was the last interesting conversation you had?”
- “I strongly believe every day is a school day. What was the last thing you learned?”
- “Tell me about your relationship with your boss.”
- “What was the last challenge you took on?”
    - “What do you think you could have done better?”

Be honest and genuine:

There is not much to it, just be honest, genuine and natural. People easily notice fake manners and they don’t feel comfortable speaking with someone who isn’t showing his or her true nature. Your sincerity will be much more appreciated than any attempts at seeming sophisticated. Keep it real and simple and just be yourself.

Remember their first name:

Pay attention to people when they introduce themselves and make sure to remember their first name. This shows that you are interested in them and that you want to build a sense of camaraderie with them.

Addressing them using their first name, after making sure that they are comfortable with it, can put them more at ease.

Forgetting someone's first name is not only embarrassing, but it can also easily insult the other person. There can be significant ramifications and it can seriously damage business relationships. Dale Carnegie once stated, "A person's name is to him or her the sweetest and most important sound in any language."

Here are a few steps to make remembering the first name a breeze:

1. **Focus solely on the person**

   The moment you meet someone, give him or her your undivided attention.

   A. Square your shoulders toward him or her,

   B. Look him or here in the eyes

   C. Shake hands

   D. Smile with your eyes

   E. Listen intently

   Learning his or her name and interacting in a meaningful way is the top priority. Avoid getting distracted and don't blame it on bad memory. In all honesty, forgetting someone's name is often caused by lack of focus and effort, rather than a brain deficiency.

2. Use their name out loud

This is basically a way to reinforce their name into your memory. You should use their name immediately after they introduce themselves and then at least one more time at the end of the conversation by thanking them.

3. Ask a question with the name

Use their name at the beginning or end of a question. This provides them an opportunity to speak, which helps store their name in your memory bank. People love hearing their own name, it's a fact. It also relays the message that you're interested in him or her and want to learn more about them.

A major pitfall is that we tend to start talking about ourselves immediately and not showing interest in the other person, which unfortunately shifts the focus away from the other person and back to us. Avoid this costly mistake by simply incorporating their name into a question.

Chapter 5: Going Beyond with the Power of Conversation

As mentioned before, assertiveness is a key element when holding conversations. It allows you to communicate your expectations and to express yourself. It helps you have a part in the discussion and establish your presence within a party of people. The influence you exert by being assertive is built on the following factors

Interaction:

Interacting with people allows us to read their body language and the subtle non-verbal cues that accompany their participation in a conversation. This, in turn, helps us understand these people and their reasoning, their likes and dislikes. This understanding can be used to your advantage by manipulating the people you are conversing with and eventually, directing the conversation to your liking.

When analyzing body language, it is important to keep in mind that these techniques will not apply to every single person 100% of the time. Factors such as culture and a person's unique body language habits must also be taken into consideration to accurately reveal nonverbal signals.

Here are a few key things to keep an eye out for:

1. Study the Eyes

Eye behavior can be very revealing. When speaking with someone, pay close attention to whether or not he or she makes direct eye contact or looks away.

The inability to make direct eye contact by looking away and to the side can signify deceit, boredom, and even disinterest. If a person looks down, on the other hand, it often indicates submissiveness or nervousness.

A. Pupil Dilation

When a person is genuinely interested and their brain is actively working to follow the conversation the pupils will dilate. For example, if someone is focused on someone or something they like, their pupils will spontaneously dilate.

It can be difficult to detect pupil dilation, however by paying attention you may be able to detect it.

B. Blinking Rate

A person's blinking rate can be a tell-tale sign of what is going on inside of them. The blinking rate will often increase when someone is actively thinking more or is stressed out. In rare occasions, frequent blinking can indicate lying when paired with touching of the eyes and mouth.

C. Glancing

Glancing at something can indicate a desire for that particular thing.

For example, if someone frequently glances at the door this could mean a desire to leave. Glancing at another person can mean a desire to talk to him or her. It is also said that looking upwards and to the right during a conversation signifies the person is lying, while on the other hand looking upwards and to the left means the person is telling the truth.

This comes down to the right side and left side of the brain to access different cognitive functions. People who look up and to the left and activating the left side of their brain which helps recall an actual memory. Those who look up and to the right are accessing the right side of their brain which tends to deal with the imagination and creative storytelling.

2. Watch the Face

People have a tendency to control their facial expressions, but if you pay close attention, you will be able to pick up on a few nonverbal signals.

The smile

There is a fake smile and a genuine smile that have completely different meanings and is important to watch for.

A genuine smile uses the entire face, whereas a fake smile only engages the mouth.

A genuine smile suggests:

- The person is happy and enjoying the company of the people around him or her.

A fake smile:

- is meant to convey pleasure or approval, but suggests that the person is actually feeling something else.

A "half-smile":

- Another common facial behavior that only uses one side or the other of the mouth which indicates sarcasm or uncertainty.

3. Proximity

Proximity is the distance between two people, or rather between the other person and you. If you want a general idea if a person views you favorably, keep an eye on how close a person sits or stands next to you. Standing or sitting close to someone else is potentially one of the best rapport indicators. Alternatively, if a person moves away when you move closer to them, this could be a strong sign that the connection is not mutual. Be very aware of proximity, because the comfort level often is very apparent when paying attention to the distance between people. Personal space can be accidentally invaded easily and create an uncomfortable situation if you do not read these important cues. This distance will vary from culture to culture so keep in mind this difference as well.

4. Mirroring

Mirroring is a powerful technique and a fundamental piece of advice given when learning to read body language.

Basically, mirroring is copying the other person's body language.

For example, while conversing with someone, pay attention to the way he or she position themselves. Perhaps they are sitting down with their hands clasped together. If a person mimics your body language, this is a clear sign that he or she is looking to create good rapport with you. When a person does something similar to us, we tend to feel more comfortable.

5. Arm positioning

The arms play an important role in body language often telling how comfortable a person is. Think of the arms as a way to safeguard the body in unknown situations.

If a person crosses their arms while communicating with you, this typically signifies as a defensive gesture. Crossed arms can also mean vulnerability, anxiety, or a closed mind. If the person has a genuine smile along with their arms crossed then it can mean a relaxed and confident attitude.

Expertise

Expertise is important because it lends you a sense of confidence. We are more comfortable speaking about something if we feel like we have a thorough knowledge of what we are talking about. Furthermore, confidence allows us to be better conversationalists. It is what enables people to be assertive in the first place.

Positional power

Positional power results in assertiveness because people who hold it know that they have the level of authority it takes to be assertive. People give deference to authority and therefore, the person wielding the positional power can easily lead and dominate a conversation.

Emotion

Humans, being emotional creatures by nature, are influenced by passion. Using your emotions when you speak to express yourself and how much you care about the subject being discussed can sway people's opinions to your advantage. It gives the impression that you are empowered by your feelings and that you are in touch with the part of yourself that makes you human. This not only makes you appear sincere, but it also makes you relatable. This is because our emotions appeal to the empathetic side in people.

Conclusion

Congratulations on making it this far! Thank you for reading this book. Now that you have learned about Small Talk, Starter topics and the Do's and Don'ts of making conversation, you are ready to go out there and practice what you have learned. Remember, the more conversations you hold, the better you will get at talking to people. Make sure to also enjoy the human bond that you will be making with your conversation partners and the knowledge you will accumulate from speaking with them. We have faith in you and encourage you to make the best of what life has to offer. Good luck!

Book 7.

Social skills

Effective techniques to improve conversations, manage your shyness, develop your charisma and how to make friends quickly

Introduction

Your palms sweaty, forehead layered with hot beads of perspiration as you stand before a crowd realizing it's your turn to speak. Frightened and overwhelmed with the thought of having that many eyes intently focused on your every single word. You know what you want to say, but you can't seem to even mutter a peep.

Public speaking can be a very daunting experience individually and even in front of large groups of people. In fact, social phobia is highly ranked in the top ten as one of the most common fears of humans. Most would rather avoid this debilitating experience altogether, but at least once in our lives we are tasked to face this fear head on. Because, the reality is, as humans we are social creatures and it is in our nature to thrive off interactions. Which is why one of the cruelest corporal punishments is solitary confinement.

A key element to having a successful life filled with meaningful relationships is to cultivate strong communication skills. Unfortunately, many suffer from shyness and a lack of charisma, ultimately having a negative impact on their self-esteem and self-image. The way we view ourselves is the way we perceive the world and what we believe to be possible. You may even know someone yourself who is a lone wolf due to their lack of social skills. Eager to leave while among a group of people or feeling awkward interacting with someone at the grocery store.

While we may not all be excessively shy or be considered introverts, sharpening your communication tools is critical to not only enjoy friends and family, but to also better prepare yourself for any opportunities that may come your way. Social skills are not something people are born with, but rather a skillset which is acquired through a variety of life experiences. The good news is that little by little you can start to layer your experiences and build off of each interaction to develop strong social skills. Realize that you are not forever stuck with being shy or not knowing how to effectively communicate with other people. In fact, it's quite the opposite, and that's the beautiful thing about it.

Perhaps you have gone through books about developing social skills which claim to have quick fixes only to find out they're plagued with vague, unactionable tips. Or maybe you scoured the internet for a solution you could actually implement, but to no avail you weren't able to find an easy-to-follow solution. With so much information it's easy to feel overwhelmed simply trying to decide which approach would be most effective for you.

Well, have it be known that this book is guaranteed to not only provide you with the resources and actionable steps to help you make gigantic strides with your confidence, but will show you how to become more relatable, communicate effectively and foster long term, meaningful relationships.

You must know, however, that simply by reading this book you will not instantly become a master of social skills, quite the contrary in fact. You will need to put into practice the tips contained in the pages to come. Commitment and dedication are critical to achieve growth and lasting results.

Positive energy attracts positive energy and the same can be said about negative energy. What we emit is what we will receive. I'm not saying this to get all woo-woo, or pretend to have some supernatural powers. But, think about it for a minute.

Positive thinking attracts even more positive thoughts to you. But it also does the same for negative thoughts, so from this point forward start paying attention to the type of thoughts you have. When they're negative thoughts, avoid marinating on them or worse, acting on them, just let them pass through.

Now is the time to take action and make the changes necessary to transform your life into an amazing one filled with the right kinds of people you so deserve. This can only begin once you make the commitment to put an end to the awkward feeling of social anxiety. What awaits you is a world full of opportunities and possibilities that you never knew existed. So, what are you waiting for? Time to take the leap!

CHAPTER 1: COMBATING SHYNESS

Before you start working on your social skills, it is important to identify the obstacles that will get in your way and know how to overcome them. One of those obstacles is shyness. As the terminology suggests, developing social skills means that you will have to be in social situations and shyness will make that very difficult for you. Shyness will come in the way of your improvement in all fields that involve human interaction: school, work, and relationships. It will prevent you from approaching people and forming meaningful bonds and connections. You must already know the negative effects of shyness on your life so here are some pointers on how you can beat it. So, let's get into it without further ado.

How to beat one on one shyness

Being in a situation where you have to face another person exclusively can be a very intimidating prospect. It can be an interview, a confrontation or simply a face to face conversation. Your shyness leads you to believe it is a threatening situation and your body reacts accordingly. Your hands may shake, you will sweat, maybe your face will redden and your breathing will quicken. Not the most appealing look to have. In order to overcome this, you have to make yourself believe that there is no danger around you. You must understand that you are safe and you have things under control and everything will be all right. Here is how you can go about doing that

1. **Take deep breaths**

When you feel that you are getting overwhelmed with anxiety in a one on one situation, take a deep relaxing breath. Inhale, keep the air in a bit longer than you usually do, then slowly exhale. This helps you calm your nerves and by slowing your breathing, you also calm your erratic heartbeat. This tells your body that things are under control and that there is no need to go into fight or flight mode.

2. **Adjust your body posture**

The way you carry yourself tells a lot about your state of mind. Hunched shoulders, bent head and crossed arms will instantly give away the fact that you are nervous. From there, it is not hard to deduce that that nervousness stems from your shyness. However, in any social situation, you want to appear confident and to do that, you will have to adjust your posture. Straighten your back, uncross your arms and raise your chin. Remember, you want to appear very comfortable with the situation. So, you have to work on any signs that you think make you seem nervous and uneasy. Being conscious of your body posture will also help you feel more confident simply by making small adjustments. In fact, researchers have even found that merely forcing a smile increases happiness and eases stress. Not to mention, a smile is nearly universally understood and transcends language barriers.

3. **Shift your focus away from you**

Being a shy person sometimes means you spend more time with your thoughts than you should and those thoughts are not always good. Sometimes, when we are in social situations our thoughts take a bad direction. They tell us that we are not good enough and that we are making a mess of things. This especially tends to happen when we are conversing with someone whom we view as superior. In order to overcome those negative thoughts, try to shift your focus from yourself to your surroundings. Better yet, focus on the person you are with. This will keep your mind from drifting to self-destructive thinking with the added bonus of appearing attentive to what the other person is telling you.

How to get your voice to be heard

Shy people tend to keep to themselves and are often very quiet. This stems from their reluctance to interact with people for fear of saying the wrong thing. When they do speak, it is usually in a low voice. If you are often asked to repeat yourself or if you see people leaning forward in order to hear you better you probably suffer from that problem. However, if you are going to get into social situations, you will need to make sure that your voice is heard. Not only will it help you communicate properly, but it will also give you an air of confidence. Here is how you can do that;

1. Take a deep breath before speaking.

2. Your voice sounds stronger if it comes from your belly. So, make sure that's where it emerges from.

3. Carefully form your words and make sure you speak them clearly.

4. Regulate your pace, do not speak too fast or too slow.

5. Try to speak across rooms more often. This will make you speak louder.

Here a few additional tips on how you can overcome your shyness

1. Pat yourself on the back

The feeling of accomplishment can be addicting. In fact, our brains naturally push us into repeating rewarding behavior. So, every time you speak to a stranger or get into social interaction, make sure to savor the success. Maybe even reward yourself with your favorite pastry. Applaud your efforts and you'll find that repeating your actions will come effortlessly after every time.

2. Learn conversation skills

Learning conversational skills will give you the confidence to interact with others more. Knowing that you already have the necessary knowledge to converse with others will make speaking to them less intimidating. This is a great way to quickly improve your social skills.

3. Practice meditation

Meditation not only helps you soothe your nerves and calm your anxiety, but it also has a resting effect on our minds. Practice meditation to drive away the negative thoughts and the self-deprecating inner dialog.

4. Physically meet with real humans

You may have no issues communicating on social media and though that can make you feel very good, you shouldn't confuse it with real-life interactions. make sure to meet real people in person and converse with them. That is what will improve your social skills. However, it won't hurt to channel the confidence you got from texting people online, it will give a confidence boost in real life.

How to get over shyness at work or at school

The school and the workplace are places where people spend the majority of their time. This means that they have to interact with the same people on a regular basis and it usually doesn't take long for those people to notice a person's shyness. Being labeled as a shy person can put you under a lot of added pressure; here is how you can cope with that pressure;

1. **Participation**

   Get involved, it is that simple. Don't wait for anyone to extend an invitation, schools and workplaces usually have organized social activities that anyone can participate in. So, go on that camping trip with your classmates or join the celebration after closing a big deal at the company. This gives you great opportunities to work on your social skills so, jump right in and interact with everyone else.

2. **Become an expert**

Being good at what you do makes you an authority in that field. People naturally gravitate towards the best person at the job to seek help or to learn from them. If you become an expert, it will lead others to interact with you without you approaching them first. This will help you improve your social skills as you will be gaining experience on how to interact with others. It will also help your confidence as you will know that you are the one to ask whenever others are facing difficulties.

3. **Deliberately put yourself out there**

No amount of reading about shyness will help you get over it if you don't get out of your comfort zone. Yes, it can be difficult but it is the only way you can make any progress. Go sit with your colleagues or classmates at lunch and maybe join the conversation. Give a presentation to report your department's progress. You can even organize an outing to get to know them better. Just do things that will allow you to interact with people and challenge your limitations. You can start with something simple like buying coffee for a colleague or sharing your notes with a classmate and then you can pick up the pace from there.

4. **Timeliness**

Being on time is something advantageous for you and not just because it is the courteous thing to do. It also saves you from having to walk into a class full of seated classmates and a teacher that does not appreciate the interruption. Shy people seldom like to be the center of attention and making an entrance will get you just that. So be on time!

CHAPTER 2: HOW TO IMPROVE YOUR CONVERSATION SKILLS

Humans, as social beings, rely mainly on conversation to communicate. This would imply that social interaction comes naturally to all human beings. Unfortunately, that is not the case. Some of us just have to work harder to develop that skill. If you often wonder what you should say next when having a conversation, you likely have that problem as well. Here are some tips to help you play your part in a conversation so that you don't have to worry about keeping it going smoothly.

Maintain flow

Pausing awkwardly now and then in a conversation shows how uncomfortable you are with the situation. Here is how you can keep the conversation going;

Avoid eliciting one-word responses

If you ask people yes or no questions or other types of questions that don't require them to elaborate, you will get one-word answers and you risk having the conversation end there. Ask questions that allow the other party to give a detailed answer. Asking "What did you do on the weekend?" will be much better for the flow of the conversation than asking "How was your weekend". That is because to answer the first question, the other party will have to enumerate a list of tasks they did. However, the second question will only prompt an answer like "Good" or "Not bad."

Don't ask superficial questions

The conversation may start with relatively shallow small talk, but if you want to make something meaningful out of it, you should take the talk to a deeper level. Stay away from superficial questions; anything like discussing the weather and traffic will not get you very far. If the other party is comfortable with it, you can even ask personal questions. Just make sure you are not just talking for the sake of it, make it count.

Share so that they also want to share

A conversation is two-sided. You shouldn't just ask endless questions without giving them some information about yourself. After a while, you will seem nosey and indiscreet and that will put them on their guard. Being open about yourself will encourage them to do the same. When they answer any questions you ask, share how you see things from your perspective about the subject.

It's ok to be vulnerable

As mentioned previously, opening up to the other party will encourage them to open up to you in turn. The more you are willing to share the more they will tell you about themselves. Here is how you can be more open when having a conversation.

Understand yourself

You will not be able to talk about your interests if you don't even know what they are. Get to know yourself. Find out what your personality is like, what your views and beliefs are and what you are passionate about. As you understand yourself, you will have the material you will need to talk about yourself. This will strengthen your self-esteem as you will get to know just how deep of a person you are.

Talk about yourself

Talking about your life, your interests, and your views will give the impression that you are willing to make a meaningful connection. When the person you are conversing with sees that you are sharing parts of yourself, they would want to do the same. This encourages the other person to talk about themselves as well and that is how the two of you will bond.

However, make sure that you don't come across as self-centered or conceited. And be sure you don't share too much about yourself at the wrong timing.

There is a fine line that must be understood while speaking about yourself.

Only speaking about yourself can create a negative impression of yourself causing people to be less interested in having another conversation or engaging with you in the future.

A quality conversation should never be one-sided, so imagine it being similar to a game of ping pong. Feel free to be genuinely curious about the other person and ask open-ended questions. After they have finished speaking you can either:

1. Provide comments about their answer

2. Ask them another question

If they're a good conversationalist they will hit the proverbial ping pong ball back your way and ask you about your thoughts on the particular topic or hopefully ask you an entirely different question. When answering their question, unless asked to fully elaborate in detail keep your answers to a high-level overview. Of course, these are simple tips to keep the conversation moving along and are not set in stone. Use them as a guide as the dynamic of the conversation continues to evolve.

Actively listening. Wait to respond

A big part of what makes a good conversationalist is their listening skills. Make sure to do your share of the talking but pay close attention to what the other person is saying.

More often than not, we as listeners want to jump right to giving out advice while the other person is still speaking. Especially when someone is feeling vulnerable, going through a difficult situation or simply blowing off steam we want to cut them off and give our input. We think to ourselves, "This person *must* be seeking my advice if they're telling me their problem!" However, in reality, most people just want to be heard and not given advice. This is the wrong approach!

When you are listening to someone, it is important that your end goal is understanding them and not giving them an answer. Make sure you pay attention to their words and be sure you are absorbing everything they are trying to tell you. Do not think about your answer while they are still speaking, wait until they are done and then take a moment to organize your thoughts before you respond. Actively listening is a crucial step to developing your social skills. Sometimes what is not said can be even more powerful than what is.

Again, it should be noted, however, that once the person is finished speaking and *asks* for your opinion, they have officially given you permission to provide advice.

Keep this in mind the next time a friend, coworker, family member or even a significant other engages with you in a conversation.

Here are a few ways you can improve your listening skills:

1. **Nod**

   Nodding along to what you are told is a sign of focus and understanding. This shows that you are paying attention to what is being said and are making the effort to follow the conversation. However, do not keep nodding non-stop as they might perceive it as you trying to pretend you are interested in what they are saying. Know when to give a validating nod at the end of each point they are making.

2. **Clarify with questions**

When you ask questions relating to what you are being told, the other party will know that you are doing your best to understand what they are saying. Do not interrupt them when they are speaking but ask a question now and then to make things clearer.

3. Repeat when necessary

After a person finishes talking about a certain point, try to repeat what they were saying in different words before you share your own views on the subject. This not only helps you make sure you understood them right, but it also shows them that you have been paying attention to what they were saying and that you are just as invested as they are in the conversation.

CHAPTER 3: HOW TO DEVELOP YOUR CHARISMA

Knowing what to do in theory and improving your skills by practicing is only part of the equation to perfect your social skills. Charisma is the other part. Being good at what you do will get people's attention but you must also be able to charm others in order to navigate your way through social life. Charisma is what makes you a memorable person. It is what makes the impact on the people you are socializing with.

Engage their attention

It is very easy to tell when someone is not giving you their full attention. They may not be interested in what you are saying or simply find your method of delivery boring. To increase your charisma, however, you also have to strengthen your presence. You have to engage others' attention and make them hang onto your every word. Here is how you can manage that;

Eye contact

Eye contact is a very powerful tool to use when you are trying to work on your charisma. It reflects your confidence, honesty and will to make a connection with the other party. It also allows you to pick up a few hints on how they are taking the conversation.

Facial expression and gestures

Facial expressions add character to your words. They make a big impact and reflect how much passion you have for your subject. Practice your facial expressions in front of a mirror or in front of a friend and see if they look weird or exaggerated. The goal is to produce facial expressions that are powerful enough to add weight to your words but natural enough to be credible.

Your words Matter

Words are extremely powerful. For over 5,000 years, humans have communicated with each other in two primary ways: speaking and writing.

With careful word choice anything can be accomplished. Your words can determine or dictate your attitude and the emotions of those around you. We all want to associate with happy, enthusiastic, fulfilled and friendly people.

Learn to read emotions

It is important to have the ability to read people's emotions and recognize them just through their gestures and facial expressions. Practice this skill by playing a mime game with a few friends. Have them act out a scene without saying anything and try to guess what is happening. You can also pick random clips from shows you don't watch and mute the sound. After that, put what you have learned into practice in real-life situations and try reading people's emotions in social settings. This will help you make deductions about other people's state of mind solely from non-verbal cues and respond accordingly.

Give undivided attention, Be present

This means giving all your attention to the person you are conversing with. Make sure you have the time to listen to them and to switch off any electronics or sources of distraction. Pay attention to them and nod every now and then to let them know you are following what they are saying.

Praise others in public

The truth is that no one receives as much praise as they'd like. The problem is that people like to talk about themselves and what they do well and get lost in their own accomplishments. If you truly want to become more charismatic, shine the spotlight on others. The reality is people love receiving praise and even more significant to them is that you cared enough to pay attention to what they do. This will not go unnoticed so, make someone's day and compliment them.

Avoid discussing the failings of others

Once in a while we may indulge in a little gossip. It's a fact of life, whether we like it or not. Sometimes the gossip is just too juicy to not lean in and listen or even participate yourself. Here's the deal, we don't tend to respect those who talk trash about others behind people's backs. This also includes laughing at people because you will inevitably lose their trust as this will lead them to wonder if you will laugh at them as well.

Affect your audience

Increasing your charisma can also be done by making an impact on your audience. Emotionally moving the people who you interact with and influencing them in some way will make them appreciate you and remember you. Here are a few ways to make a lasting impression of those around you in social situations.

1. **Poise**

   Stay calm and composed. You want to look dignified and graceful and that will be expressed through your body language, tone, and expressions. Speak clearly and make sure you don't stutter at any point in your speech. Don't fidget or move too much. Remember, you want to seem perfectly put together.

2. **Knowledge breeds confidence**

   Being an educated person will always earn you a certain air of confidence. Which is why you should strive to accumulate as much knowledge as you can about all kinds of things; your work, your hobbies, your culture and even things that don't interest you. Having this knowledge will boost your confidence and that will make an impact on the people around you.

3. **Composure**

   Posing is another subtle way to look charismatic. You know how movie stars always strike poses when alighting from their cars and ooze confidence in the face of tens of flashing cameras. You should look up poses that express your authority and use them when interacting with others. Putting your hands in your pockets may give away your shyness if you do it wrong but if you stand confidently and relax your shoulders it can reflect your comfort in your surroundings.

4. **Less is more, Talk less**

Talking too much tells people that you are insecure and have something to prove. Put value in your words and only say what is necessary. Do not speak too fast and make sure you properly articulate. There is something to be said about meticulously selecting words that are eloquently stated. Words are powerful, choose them wisely.

Be quick to admit your failures

I want you to think about this for a second, if Superman were to be invincible and didn't have any weaknesses would he be that interesting?

Probably not. You see, because Superman has a weakness to kryptonite he is more "human", more relatable, and we can see ourselves sharing his experiences. When you share your weaknesses, people will be able to far relate to you better, see you for who you are and learn from your mistakes. When you make fun of yourself, people won't be laughing at you, but rather laughing *with* you.

So, remember to stay humble, be quick to admit your failures and you'll see how much more people will enjoy being in your presence.

Managing awkwardness

When interacting with others, feeling out of place might lead us to behave awkwardly. This awkwardness may be endearing in some cases but it doesn't help when you are trying to become more charismatic. Here are some tips that can help you get rid of the unwanted awkwardness and improve your charisma:

1. **Socialize more**

   Though being in social situations and behaving awkwardly may feel embarrassing, there is no better way to improve. Learn how to repress the awkward behavior and interact with people to practice the solutions you came up with. You will see that your clumsiness will have decreased after a few social interactions. The more often you socialize the more comfortable you will become.

2. **Stop worrying about your behavior**

   Worrying about how awkward you are will only make things worse. By fretting over the issue, you will get even more nervous and become more susceptible to act awkwardly. Instead, relax and act naturally. Avoid thinking that you are an awkward person and tell yourself that you have things under control and that it will go just fine. Positive thoughts! Remember, if you consciously make the decision that a particular situation is not awkward, it will not be awkward. This truly comes down to not only framing the situation in a positive way, but having a strong mindset.

3. Fitness

Just as important as it is to strengthen your mental fitness, becoming physically fit is an excellent way skyrocket your confidence and to drive away any insecurities you may have about your appearance. No doubt it will make you feel more confident about yourself. Additionally, physical activity helps you relax and work out any nervousness. Being in good shape will not only have a positive impact on your state of mind, but clearly it is also good for your health.

I'm not saying you need to become a gym rat, run a marathon or a triathlete, but even incorporating a little more physical activity in your life will do wonders for your confidence. Give it a shot.

Caution: Becoming physically fit may have a significant positive impact on your life expectancy, which is pretty cool.

Conclusion

Congratulations, you have now made it to the end of the book! Now that you are better equipped to have meaningful interactions in social settings it is time to test your newly acquired knowledge. Get involved in social gatherings and interact with people. Speak to strangers and pay attention to all the crucial feedback you will learn from practicing in each new engagement. Keep track of your progress and remember to acknowledge your efforts and reward yourself. Good luck!

Book 8.

Cognitive Behavioral Therapy

Easy and Effective Strategies to Rewire Your Brain - Overcome Depression, Phobias and Anxiety using Highly Effective Psychological Techniques

Introduction

In the 1960s a psychiatrist by the name of Aaron Beck made a profound observation during analytical sessions that his patients often had an internal dialogue in their minds at the same time. This internal dialogue was a conversation to themselves that was never spoken about out loud. What eventually was discovered was that this conversation or series of thoughts also had a significant impact on their emotions.

During a typical session Beck may be intently listening to the patient, however he would not be giving much feedback apart from a slight nod here and there. Meanwhile, the patient may be thinking to themselves, "He's been awfully quiet during this session. I wonder if he's upset with me?" These thoughts alone could make the patient feel unsure, anxious and a slew of other negative emotions. Inside the patient's mind the internal conversation might continue, "He might be exhausted. I know he just had a newborn and perhaps he was up all night." Suddenly, this internal thought would cause a shift in the patient's emotions and make them go from anxious to calm.

It was this revelation which led Beck to discover the strong correlation between our thoughts and our emotions or feelings. He began to expand on this concept and soon after, he coined the term automatic thoughts, which are emotion-filled thoughts that occur suddenly.

Additionally, Beck came to realize that not everyone took notice of these thoughts and how they affected their feelings, but with some practice they could develop the ability to identify and track them.

What happens is, when a person is in any given situation, there is a continued thread of thoughts that go through their mind, in fact, these are the thoughts that were mentioned above as automatic thoughts. Those same thoughts change accordingly to fit the change of the situation that the individual is experiencing. Those thoughts are highly influenced by the beliefs of the person and their past experiences in life and when the situation falls out of the individual's comfort zone, they take a negative turn. He came to the conclusion that targeting these thoughts was the key component to the patient understanding and combating his or her challenges. If someone was feeling upset in some way, the underlying thoughts were often negative and were neither helpful nor realistic. But, addressing these thoughts as they come up makes it much easier to manage the emotions that soon follow.

The idea of managing emotions might sound foreign to you as you perhaps believe that how you feel is out of your hands and that your emotions cannot be controlled. While this might be partly true, there is more to it than that. In other words, while you cannot instantly alter your feelings or switch them off, it is still possible for you to make your emotions of a more positive, or at least reasonable nature by managing your actual thoughts.

This works because contrary to your emotions, your thoughts are something that you can control. You can decide at any time to start thinking about something else or to change the nature of your thoughts. Similarly, you have full control over your actions and behaviors. By transition, you have an indirect type of control over your feelings. You know that this is true because you have been through it before. You must have gone through a situation in which you decided to get your mind off of a stressful thought by watching a movie or going out for a walk. You also tell yourself to think of something else when you are upset. This is because you are unconsciously aware that your thoughts and actions impact your emotions.

As the therapy encompasses behavioral techniques and also places an emphasis on thinking, Beck deemed it to be Cognitive Behavioral Therapy.

As the saying goes, "Whether you think you can or you think you can't, you're right." Think about that for a second.

We all have limiting beliefs and it's these same core beliefs that shackle us from progression. In fact, once you realize that it's not specific events that upset us, but the meanings and value we give them, your radical transformation can begin.

If your thoughts are too negative, they can block your ability to see things for their true potential. Put another way, we continue to hold on to the same old thoughts and belief patterns and fail to learn anything new, which stymies our growth.

CBT is a powerful tool that if used correctly can completely change the way you view life. If you don't believe me, look no further than Roger Bannister who broke the 4-minute mile barrier on May 6th, 1954. It is said that for thousands of years runners had tried to break this threshold, but to no avail. Experts came to the conclusion that the body was simply not capable of enduring this feat, deeming it impossible and too dangerous. You see, Roger Bannister not only trained physically for this accomplishment, but also mentally. He had visualized this feat every day, making certain that he would, without a doubt, be victorious.

However, as amazing as this is, what's even more impactful and important to understand are the effects of this achievement on us as humans. No more than a year later, several people broke the 4-minute mile as well! A paradigm shift took place and positive thought patterns paved the way to achieve the impossible. Once people saw that someone else was able to do it, they were able to as well!

What this unveils is that we are what we think, it's as simple as that. When you have unshakable conviction, intense focus and every cell in your body believes in something without a doubt, the magic will begin to manifest. Realize that this approach of thought patterns and mental framing spans much further than simply breaking records. Cognitive Behavioral Therapy strives to address a wide range of challenges such as mood disorders, anxiety disorders, psychotic disorders, eating disorders, substance abuse and even performance enhancements.

The following pages in this book will help you navigate the world of Cognitive Behavioral Therapy with actionable tips to help you become the best version of yourself. You will discover a series of helpful and enlightening exercises that can have a tremendous and positive impact on your life, but it's up to you to take massive action.

If you're ready to take a leap of faith and see how confronting your challenges head on can change your life then flip the page right now and figure out how you can go about it. You can do it! Good luck.

CHAPTER 1. WHAT IS COGNITIVE BEHAVIORAL THERAPY?

A form of psychotherapeutic treatment, cognitive behavioral therapy or CBT is a short-term therapy technique that helps patients understand their thoughts and feelings in order to fix problems and improve mental health.

CBT considers thoughts as the basis of feeling. What you think directly impacts your emotions. It considers that even though we cannot change our circumstances and variables which are out of our control, we can change our thoughts in a way that allows us to make the best of any situation. In theory, it considers that particular situations lead to particular thoughts which then lead to particular feelings. These feelings, if unpleasant, can turn into anxiety and mood disorders.

The fact that feelings are hard to control and alter, CBT focuses on changing the thoughts which it considers the roots of these feelings, and as its name suggests, cognitive behavioral therapy is a combination of cognitive therapy and behavioral therapy. The first focuses on analyzing and working on thoughts and the second is a behavior-oriented approach. In simpler words, CBT is about what you think and do. It helps you change the negative and inaccurate way of thinking in order to develop a better, clearer and more effective response mechanism to events.

Why Cognitive Behavioral Therapy?

CBT is a research-based treatment supported by numerous studies and scientific evidence. It has proven to be effective in treating depression, anxiety, eating disorders and other conditions. It can also help a person move on from a loss, cope with drastic changes and accept loss.

Since it helps you manage your feelings and behaviors by changing your thoughts, CBT allows you to develop a better outlook of life as it will focus on positive feelings and behaviors.

How does it work?

CBT can be obtained through one on one sessions with a therapist but it can also be delivered in group sessions, through books and manuals and even online.

Regardless of how you go about it, in order for cognitive behavioral therapy to work, you must be willing to talk about your feelings. Therefore, if you are usually reluctant about discussing your emotions, it might not be the best remedy and you should seek out alternative solutions.

However, if speaking about your feelings is not a challenge for you, definitely give it a shot!

Though your therapist will help you find out what you should be dealing with, it can be helpful to review your issues in advance. Try to actively pay attention to your thoughts and take note each time you catch yourself having negative thoughts. Make a list of those thoughts and try to write a couple of sentences on why they bother you and what triggers them. For instance, if you are in a café and spill your cup of coffee, you might think to yourself something along the lines of “I'm such a klutz! I'm worthless!” Negative thoughts will creep into your mind about the inconvenience you’ve made for the waiter and you will be blaming yourself for all sorts of things while in reality, it was just an accident that you blew out of proportion. However, for the waiter this is a common occurrence and those in the café will most likely smile sympathetically at you for a moment before turning back to their work or conversation. What happened is, the surprise of having to deal with something that you weren't expecting and the embarrassment that you felt lead you to have those negative thoughts about yourself.

The therapy session

Your therapist will be asking questions relating to your thoughts and emotions and will try to determine what is troubling you. It might be difficult at first, but they will help you become more comfortable as the session progresses.

You will be asked to put into practice what you learn from each therapy session. Additionally, it wouldn't be out of the ordinary for your therapist to suggest some reading materials or ask you to keep a journal so you can keep track of your thoughts, feelings and behaviors. A journal is a very effective way to help you see the progress you make.

Chapter 2. The Cognitive Behavioral Model

Understanding the cognitive behavioral model will give you more insight into CBT. This is a theory in the psychological field that details the concept in which thoughts, feelings and behaviors are related. While it is common belief that the feelings we experience stem from the daily situations that we go through, there is actually more to it than that. The fact that different people feel differently about the same situation proves this. While some people might feel nervous before a long race, others feel excited.

The cognitive behavioral model states that it isn't the situation that sparks the feeling but rather what we think about the situation. Those thoughts are what trigger those feelings depending on their nature. People who suffer from depression and anxiety tend to have a negative thought process following certain situations. The thought patterns that they have are usually distorted, pessimistic and are often times blown out of proportions. The negative emotions that they experience afterwards are a direct result to what they are thinking. If someone fails a certain task and feels worthless, that emotion is caused by thoughts such as "I am so stupid", "I can't believe I messed up so bad" and "I can't get anything right". Needless to say, that these thoughts are inaccurate and exaggerated as one failed task hardly makes a person stupid or good for nothing.

The goal of CBT is to teach you to reform the thoughts that trigger the negative feelings you often experience after a certain situation. Since avoiding certain situations entirely may not always be possible, CBT teaches you to focus your effort on something that you can directly control: your very own thoughts. This process is the "cognitive" part of Cognitive Behavioral Therapy.

The second aspect relates to the impact that your behavior has on your mood. It helps you increase the behaviors that make you feel good and therefore have a positive impact on your mood while minimizing any behaviors associated with a negative mood. Much like the cognitive aspect, the behavioral aspect of CBT urges you to work on aspects of you that you can control, in this case: your actions and behavior.

There are three levels of thoughts and beliefs encompassed in cognitive theory: automatic thoughts, assumptions and core beliefs.

Automatic thoughts are considered the first level. They essentially are the thoughts that constantly flow through our minds about ourselves and other people. They are directed by the situations we find ourselves in throughout the day and change with the shifting of those situations. We are not always aware of them but we still feel the emotions they produce. These types of thoughts often take a negative direction as they magnify the importance of threats and risks and undermine our ability to handle the situation and problem solve. They are sometimes dysfunctional as a result of a distorted view that we have of ourselves, others and the world. However, we still take them as valid thoughts and accept them. People who suffer from depression or anxiety can experience these thoughts more acutely. It is possible to identify toxic automatic thoughts and replace them with more reasonable and positive ones.

Assumptions, also known as intermediate beliefs, represent the second level of thoughts. They are relative to our views about the world. Contrarily to automatic thoughts, they are not tied to specific situations. These thoughts are a generalization that results from a person's processing of information around them. An individual's thoughts are directly impacted by these beliefs and these thoughts will eventually have their own impact on the person's behaviors. Assumptions can be distorted much like automatic thoughts, however. For instance, beliefs such as having a certain physical appearance can lead to popularity or wearing designer clothes will earn a person respect and deference are often flawed.

The last level of thoughts is core beliefs. These thoughts are formed in our childhood and are then cemented by our perception of things as we grow older. Though they are generalized and considered as absolute by people, they may not always be right. People are more receptive to what reinforces and confirms the existence of their core beliefs, ignoring whatever may contradict them and this makes core beliefs difficult to alter. Distorted core beliefs can lead to dysfunctional assumptions and negative thoughts. Beliefs are tightly linked to an individual's accomplishments and their relationship with others.

Both assumptions and core beliefs can be challenged and altered with the same method used to alter automatic thoughts.

The three levels of thoughts are related.

The following model illustrates how:

Core beliefs → assumptions → automatic thoughts (generated by a situation) → emotions

What this means is that core beliefs impact assumptions, which in turn impact automatic thoughts that arise with any given situation and those thoughts, finally result in emotions.

There is another model used in this case called the ABC model.

A stands for Activating event, B for Beliefs and C for Consequences (emotional and behavioral consequences). This model implies that an activating event triggers a thought process and not an emotion. The emotions are actually caused by that thought process and this is more empowering because while it is sometimes impossible to alter events and situations, it is within our power to change our thoughts and beliefs.

Once you get started with CBT, the first thing you will learn is how to recognize and identify dysfunctional automatic thoughts. Once you identify the negative thoughts, you will be able to challenge them and alter them which in turn will result in more positive emotions. After that, you will be able to identify the assumptions and core beliefs which have shaped these negative automatic thoughts. Once that happens, you can focus your attention on changing those core beliefs and assumptions and by doing that, you would have handled the problem from the roots.

Making CBT effective

In order for CBT to work for you, you must have the right attitude. You have to be positive and believe that you will succeed in making a change. Your motivation to make a difference in your life and your faith in the CBT approach will make it most likely to benefit you.

Another thing that will help you with CBT is to have clear goals. CBT works best when the issues it deals with are clear whether they are fears or specific patterns of toxic thinking. Having a clearly outlined plan with specific goals will help your progress and will allow you to keep track of your growth. You can then make the proper adjustments if you deem your progress too slow or if you think you can take things to a higher level.

You will also need to invest time and effort in your journey. CBT will require you to do a number of activities like reading, journaling and facing situations that take you out of your comfort zone. This is a big part of the CBT process and will be necessary for you to see any changes.

Though it is important for you to push yourself through the activities that you will need to accomplish, be sure to take care of yourself in the process. You owe yourself kindness, respect, honesty and acceptance. Do not be judgmental toward yourself no matter what happens and remember that the fact that you are taking action to improve yourself is an achievement in and of itself.

Journaling will be a very important part of your journey. The thought journal will be used to record any problems, obstacles, goals and solutions. It will help you identify negative thoughts, the power to address them and will directly involve you in the healing process.

Monitoring progress

It is very important that you keep track of your progress when working with CBT. You must document your mood as well as your activities and, of course, your achieved goals. You are not expected to note progress immediately, it may take a week or so. However, you can make any changes that you deem necessary to help you through your journey. For instance, you can revise your goals in case you think they are too insignificant or unreasonable. Know that it's ideal to go at a pace that will help your growth and healing process. You are expected to work on behavioral-activating activities that push you forward but that you will still be able to achieve. It is also important that you are interested in the said activities. Make sure that any obstacles that you have documented are approached in a way that will not slow down your advancement. Though it is important to challenge yourself, remember that CBT is supposed to help you heal smoothly. It is not supposed to make you uncomfortable or worsen your anxiety symptoms in any way. Be particularly mindful of this if you are not working with a professional. If anything causes you discomfort, stop the activity. You may also need to stop self-directed CBT and seek help from a therapist.

Chapter 3. Approaching CBT Step by step

Step 1: Identifying the problem

Like most aspects of life, Identifying the problem is the first step you should take when you are working on yourself with the CBT approach. It might be a behavior, a feeling or a triggering thought. Regardless of what it is, it is upsetting to you and must be addressed.

In the following pages, we will address two types of upsetting thoughts: automatic thoughts and intrusive thoughts. These two categories of thoughts are very common and are often symptoms of mental disorders like post-traumatic stress disorder, obsessive-compulsive disorder and depression. It is therefore imperative that you learn more about them and learn how to recognize them.

What are automatic thoughts?

Automatic thoughts are the thoughts that occur to us effortlessly during or after any given situation as an instinctive response. They are quick to form and are usually short. They don't require any logical reasoning process or any kind of deep reflection. However, we accept them as reasonable thoughts. Though some automatic thoughts are indeed reasonable, others are not and those are known as "dysfunctional automatic thoughts".

Automatic thoughts are a very important variable in the CBT process which is why it is very important to develop the ability to identify them. In order to gain this skill, you have to be more aware of your thoughts. It is important to pay extra attention because the quickness and shortness that characterizes automatic thoughts makes it easy for them to slip by us. However, they do leave their trail in the form of resulting negative emotions. Whenever you sense an upsetting emotion, try to remember what thought had caused it. Thoughts that cause a quick shift of mood in you are often related to core beliefs and you have to make sure to take note of those. For instance, you might be out with friends and notice someone in a suit exiting a luxurious car and think to yourself "I will never be able to afford a car like that" or "That man is so much more successful than I am." Thoughts like those are dysfunctional automatic thoughts.

After identifying a situation that triggers upsetting emotions, there are some questions that you have to ask yourself in order to identify what thoughts and beliefs are behind the negative feelings that you want to get rid of.

1. What was I doing before I felt that way?
2. Where was I when those feelings occurred? Are there places where they don't occur?
3. How was I behaving just before I felt like that?
4. What was I thinking about before I started feeling that way?
5. Are those feelings intensified by any of my beliefs?
6. Who was with me when I experienced those feelings?
7. Do those feelings occur with everyone?

As stated before, automatic thoughts can be hard to keep track of because of how fast they occur and change in the span of a few seconds. Once you learn to be aware of those thoughts, you can deal with them in many different ways. If you manage to identify a particular thought and you feel that it is the one that provokes the negative emotions, focus on it. And as you pay more attention and feel that another thought causes those same emotions more intensely, redirect your efforts on that one instead. Similarly, if you believe that the problem caused by those thoughts come second to other issues, rearrange your priorities and address the thoughts that you believe are the most critical and have a worse impact on your mood.

Dysfunctional thoughts are caused by cognitive distortions, those are "thought traps" that are actually mistakes that we make during the thought process. Cognitive distortions are classified into different categories and it can be very helpful to know under which category your dysfunctional automatic thoughts fall in order to deal with them properly.

Catastrophizing

Thinking of the worst-case scenario as the final outcome of a certain situation. For instance, "If I am late to work, I'll get fired without a recommendation and I'll never find another job."

All-or-nothing

Having an extreme view of life. It is either all good or all bad, and anything in-between is unlikely to happen. "If I don't get an A on a test, I'm a failure."

Personalization

Assuming that any negative behavior, negative words from others or even a negative outcome of a situation is your fault or is caused by you when it is actually not related to you in anyway.

Over Generalizations

Projecting the negative outcome of a situation onto all situations of the same nature.

Labeling

Putting negative labels on ourselves or others. For instance, labeling yourself as a failure because of one shortcoming rather than working on it and improving yourself.

Magnification / Minimization

Belittling your achievements and strengths and blowing your failures out of proportion. In other words, focusing on the negatives and ignoring the positives.

Emotional reasoning

Allowing your feelings about a certain situation to dictate your perception of the said situation. For instance, "I feel like I have ruined things beyond repair, so my life must be ruined."

Discounting positives

Dismissing any positive experiences that contradict our negative beliefs. For instance, crediting your success on a lucky coincidence or dismissing any compliments you get from others as an effort to be polite on their part.

Negativity bias

Focusing on the bad aspects of a situation and emphasizing them and ending up seeing the situation under a completely negative light, even if it might have had some positive aspect to it.

Should / Must statements:

This pertains to imposing unrealistic expectations on yourself. Things that you think you should or must do and that leave you feeling guilty or frustrated in case they are not fulfilled. Marking the tasks you wish to accomplish as absolute and leaving no room for failure or any kind of flexibility can make things even more difficult for you as they turn into tasks you have no desire to do or that you derive no joy from.

Jumping to conclusions

The tendency to predict the worst possible outcome without any indication or evidence. For instance, predicting that a future event will have a negative outcome and acting as if the worst had already happened. Another example of jumping to conclusions is thinking that other people have perceived you in a negative light without asking them in person what they think of you.

These kinds of dysfunctional automatic thoughts can be very troublesome albeit very common. If you believe that you are struggling with these types of thoughts, make sure to include dealing with them as a part of your CBT healing process.

Defining Intrusive Thoughts

Like automatic thoughts, intrusive thoughts are very common. As their appellation suggests, these thoughts are also very upsetting. They can be somber, bad and scary and make us uncomfortable or sickened. People often say that these thoughts are not compatible with who they are as a person. However, these thoughts still occur to us unwillingly and they can be very hard to control or discard.

Intrusive thoughts are not only distressing, they can interrupt our thought process and activities and unbalance our productivity. These thoughts have been known to be symptoms of anxiety disorder, obsessive-compulsive disorder or post-traumatic stress disorder but it is possible for them to occur independently of other mental ailments.

There are many types of intrusive thoughts such as obsessional intrusions, worry intrusions and trauma-related intrusions. Each one of these types can be addressed with CBT.

Examples of intrusive thoughts

- **Worry intrusions** - Excessive concern over contracting a disease and dying
- **Trauma-related intrusions** - Random recollections about a traumatic or embarrassing event from your childhood
- **Obsessive intrusions** - The fear of losing faith in your religion or that you are practicing it incorrectly
- **Obsessional intrusions** - Unwanted sexual thoughts involving a coworker, a family member, a child or even an animal
- **Worry intrusions -** Intense doubt and insecurity concerning your performance on an exam that you have prepared for
- **Trauma-related intrusions** - Repeated recollections of a violent or upsetting event that you experienced as an adult
- **Obsessional intrusions** - Thoughts of committing violent or criminal acts like harming a loved one or killing your significant other
- **Obsessive intrusions** - The fear of losing control over what you say in public

Of course, these are only a few examples of intrusive thoughts. Many people can experience similar thoughts and it will reassure you to know that if you are experiencing them, you are not the only one. Intrusive thoughts are more common than you might think, they are not something only you have to deal with and they are certainly not a personal failing of yours.

Everyone experiences intrusive thoughts. The levels of intensity vary but studies conducted in multiple countries have shown that all people have these thoughts. The difference is not only found in the degrees of intensity, it also manifests itself in how different individuals deal with intrusive thoughts. The people who are not as bothered by them are mainly more adept at dismissing these unsettling and often disturbing thoughts and viewing them as meaningless and insignificant as opposed to others who place a great level of importance to these thoughts and manage to convince themselves that they are manifestations of their own character and nature.

It is important for you to keep in mind that just because you are having intrusive thoughts, it does not mean that you want to act on it or that you will do so at any time. They have nothing to do with how good or bad you are and they are not indicative of any future outcome for you.

Make sure to include intrusive thoughts in your problem description. You will see how CBT will help you deal with these thoughts in step 4.

Defining the problem

You are supposed to make a list of all the problems and issues you believe should be addressed with the CBT approach.

List the most important problems and note their frequency and level of severity. Make sure to include a few lines to describe how these problems impact your life.

For instance, if you experience a feeling of worthlessness, note down how many days per week you get this feeling. Try to describe the feeling precisely: frustration, anger, sadness, hopelessness, etc. Make sure to include how severe it is. Is it upsetting? Or more intensely distressing? Does it keep you from performing your daily tasks?

Problems also include symptoms of stress like insomnia, loss of appetite or overeating, so make sure you also take note of any such issues in order to work on resolving them.

Step 2: setting goals

Since you have identified and described the problems, you can now move on to the next step which is setting your goals.

You have to clearly set the goals you hope to achieve with CBT. They are supposed to be specific, measurable and most importantly, achievable. Give priority to the goals that you believe are the most important and that should be worked on first. Any goal you set has to mean something to you and to have some level of importance. If any of the goals you have set feels unimportant, change it or refine it in order for you to have the motivation to work on it later on. Make sure that the goal you have set is not vague or generic like "Feel less anxious" and instead, set goals that will directly result in that one big goal. For instance, "Meditate for 10 minutes for five days each week", "Talk to people three times", or "Listen to soothing music when walking / commuting to work".

It is also important that these goals can be measured so that you can observe the changes that are occurring and keep track of your progress. This will keep you going and boost your motivation in addition to keeping you informed of whether or not your goals are realistic, too difficult or too easy.

And lastly, make sure that your goals are realistic and reasonable. Do not set goals that require a dramatic effort from the beginning. For instance, if we take the same social anxiety example from above, notice how the suggested goals are reasonable and transitory. Do not try something like throwing a huge party or public speaking from the start. It's all about starting slow and gradually increasing your efforts. Setting unrealistic goals can cause a drop in morale in case you fail and may even have traumatic repercussions that will cause your state to worse. If you want to set ambitious goals, make sure you set them for the long term and that you have short and medium term goals that will lead up to those goals. Just take the time you need and work at your own pace.

Once you have listed your goals, you have to describe the steps that will come into play for achieving them. Always within the same social anxiety example, here are a few steps that may lead to the desired outcome:

- Practice meditation three times this week.
- Learn three ways to control physical symptoms of social anxiety this month.
- Reconnect with two people that I used to know this month.

When you note down your goals, make sure you are very specific and to include the estimated time frame.

Step 3: Identifying obstacles

Identifying the problem and setting goals are not all there is to CBT, however. You are also supposed to identify any obstacles that can get in the way of your healing process and hinder your progress.

There are many obstacles that you can encounter. For instance, the lack of a support network. Family and friends can be very helpful when you are going through any therapeutic process and CBT is no exception. When those people are not available or willing to lend their support, it can be a challenge having them nearby. Not only that, sometimes the people around us behave in a certain way that doesn't benefit the changes we are trying to make in our life which is another challenge in and of itself. Finances and the lack of funds can also be a challenge that you would have to work around as well as any impractical circumstances like bad weather or heavy traffic that can keep you from going to events. A tight schedule and lack of time is another challenge that you will have to get creative about. There are other obstacles that are less evident like drops in motivation, a perfectionist streak or low self-esteem that can keep you from achieving your goals and may result in you wanting to give up.

Challenges and obstacles are present in every endeavor. They are things that we have to deal with no matter what we do. In fact, they make things more interesting and, in a way, more fun. It is important that you don't let the prospect of facing challenges in your CBT journey intimidate you. Take your time and make your way forward. The beginning is the hardest part and as you get used to the process, things will become easier. Remember, an object in motion stays in motion. All you have to do is get the ball rolling.

Taking the time to rid your mind of negative thoughts and adopting a more positive attitude is very important and will help you through. Do not be too harsh on yourself and remind yourself that mistakes are nothing but opportunities to learn and improve. Congratulate and reward yourself for every victory and every achieved goal.

Make a list of any obstacles you believe you might need to overcome and below each item, write down anything that can potentially help you overcome those obstacles or even avoid them altogether. These will be your strategies to deal with these obstacles.

Step 4: Confronting automatic and intrusive thoughts

Identifying automatic and intrusive thoughts (Step 1) is a prerequisite to this step. Now that you have a better knowledge of the dysfunctional thoughts that are causing your problems, it is time to do something about them. This is what you will learn about in step 4.

How to combat dysfunctional automatic thoughts

The end goal is to challenge core beliefs and that happens through a gradual process that starts with challenging automatic thoughts.

Automatic thoughts are the ones that are directly behind any feelings of anxiety and extreme fear. They may be unrealistic and exaggerated but the people who have to deal with these thoughts cannot just put a stop to them through sheer willpower. It is important to remember that we have formed thought patterns through years of distorted thinking and changing them will take time, effort, determination, and most importantly, patience.

A thought journal will be a necessary asset when you get into the process of challenging your negative thoughts. You will write the three main things that come into play: the situation, the emotions, and the thoughts. You are supposed to do this for every entry. Since a specific situation is what leads to a negative emotion, you will start by describing that. Focus on situations that lead to the most intense emotional responses and describe the context and the nature of the situation. You mainly want to include what happened, when, where and with whom you were with when you experienced it. Then, note what emotions you felt and describe how severely you felt them. For instance, a "slight feeling of worry" or "An intense fear". Lastly, write down the automatic thoughts that occurred to you in that particular situation. Try to remember as many of those thoughts as possible and try to identify the specific thought that triggered the negative emotional response that you have experienced. To make this process easier, try asking yourself questions like "What was the worst thing I imagined then?", "What does it represent?" and, "What fears or worries did it trigger?". Additionally, you can include the intensity of your belief in those automatic thoughts. Repeat this exercise two to three times every day.

After identifying the automatic thought that causes you discomfort or distress, you can challenge it by taking two essential steps:

Firstly, you have to make a list of evidence (or arguments, if you will) for and against the thought in question. This list will help you understand why you are having that thought and why that thought may be exaggerated and unfounded. Ask yourself questions like "How would another person view this?", "Why do I think this way?", "Why might this not be true?", "What would I think if a loved one had the same thought about themselves?"

The list that you will be making has to be based on facts and objective reasoning. Try to put your own beliefs, views, and feelings aside as they can mislead you.

For instance, you might be worried about expressing a different opinion when you are debating a subject with a friend. You might think that they were offended or hurt and will start avoiding you. However, when you take a moment to think about it rationally and when you start gathering evidence, you can remember the fact that you and your friend parted ways on friendly terms and that they even invited you to hang out with them in a few days. It will also be helpful for you to remember that you have known this person for a long time and you have had many other disagreements with them. You also must know that disagreeing with others is not a bad thing. This process will eventually lead you to the conclusion that the negative thoughts you had originate from a deeper fear of being left alone or losing your loved ones. These emotions you have felt are not actually related to the difference in opinions that you experienced in that situation.

This separation of thoughts can be made more apparent if you view them from the lens of your already existing beliefs. Religion, for instance. Many religions teach you to let go of anger, to forgive, to give back and a lot of other virtuous behaviors. If you are religious, do not hesitate to replace negative automatic thoughts with the concepts that are a part of your faith. For instance, there are religions that urge you to repent and to learn from your mistakes to be a better person. That means that, according to your beliefs, you are supposed to make mistakes and that you should use them as opportunities to learn. There are always second chances for you to make up for your failures.

After you manage to come up with an alternative thought, make sure to assess it. Is it believable? If the answer is no, you will have to discard it and think of something better, another reasonable thought that is based on the evidence you collected in the first step. The key for it to be believable is to make it realistic. Then, once you manage to get the right level of believability, examine the emotion that results from this new thought. It is alright if there is still some negativity to it, as long as you manage to significantly decrease the intensity of it.

Although thought journaling is a very helpful and necessary part of the CBT process, it can still leave you feeling a bit bad. If you still feel the same emotionally after a session of describing your thoughts and coming up with alternatives, you can try to investigate the reason why.

For instance, it might be because you were focusing on the wrong situation. The strong negative feelings that you experienced may not have been caused by the situation and the thoughts that you were working on when you were journaling since it didn't change your emotional state. Take a second look at the emotions and thoughts that you had listed before and see if there is a thought that triggers the upsetting emotions with a greater intensity. If there is such a thought, redo the thought journaling process with it.

Another reason why you may still feel poorly might be your alternative thoughts. The thoughts that you came up with to replace the old distorted one may not fit the situation or may not be that believable and therefore, your mind might have rejected them if it viewed them as such. Reassess that thought and try to add more to the evidence that backs it up in order to make it more sensible. If that still doesn't work, abandon that particular thought and try to come up with a new alternative thought that will fit better.

Now, if nothing seems wrong with the situation and the thought, it may simply be a matter of time. Be patient and give yourself the time to adjust to the process of journaling and after a few sessions, it may work better and lead you to the desired results.

If all the solutions mentioned above do not make a difference, then it may be time to address the root of the problem. If your mind is having trouble parting with a distorted automatic thought, it is probably because it is tightly linked to a dysfunctional assumption or core belief which will require you to address your thought process on those two levels to make a change. You will learn more about that in the next step.

Recap: Keeping a thought journal

1. Identify the specific situation that triggered negative emotions and add a detailed description of it.
2. Make a list of the emotions that you experienced and include the level of intensity they were felt.
3. List the automatic thoughts that were running through your head at the time you felt the negative emotions and make sure to write how strong your belief in those thoughts were.
4. Investigate the thoughts and try to identify any cognitive distortions in them.
5. Write down evidence for and against the most intense negative thoughts.
6. Come up with a realistic, evidence-based alternative thought to replace the distorted automatic thoughts and assess its believability. If it doesn't seem believable enough, come up with a new alternative thought.
7. Reassess the emotions you felt initially and rate their intensity after the thought-journaling process. Write it in your thought journal.
8. Try the previously mentioned strategies if you feel like there has been no change after a few sessions of journaling.

Chapter 4. How To Handle Intrusive Thoughts

Now that we have been through automatic thoughts and how you can deal with them, it is time to move on to intrusive thoughts and manage them accordingly.

What makes intrusive thoughts different from automatic thoughts is the fact that they don't stem from assumptions or core beliefs, in fact, there is no clear source to them. Intrusive thoughts are as random as they are unwanted. This means that they have to be dealt with differently as well. As stated before, intrusive thoughts have nothing to do with your views, principles or beliefs, fortunately. CBT can help you manage these intrusive thoughts as well as the negative emotions and anxieties that they trigger.

Positive self-talk

This is a great way to assuage your fears regarding the intrusive thoughts that you have and to limit their impact on your emotional state. Take a moment to remind yourself that these thoughts have nothing to do with you as a person. They don't reflect your morals nor who you are as a person. They are just random thoughts and though they are disturbing, they mean nothing. Tell yourself that although you cannot control your thoughts, you have full control over your actions and that you have no wish to act on these thoughts, rendering them completely void of any deeper meaning. The fact that you find them so disturbing tells you all you need to know about your stance regarding these thoughts.

Take a moment and think about how you would respond if you found out that a loved one is struggling with these thoughts. You would clearly reassure them and tell them that these thoughts do not reflect them as a person, that these thoughts are meaningless, and that they are good and kind. You may also tell them that many people deal with intrusive thoughts and that they are more common than they think. You would also let them know that you understand and relate with them and you will tell them not to give much importance to these thoughts and to discard them. Now, with that same kindness, empathy, and compassion, tell yourself the same thing.

Accept and Move On

In order to diminish the power that intrusive thoughts have on you, you have to accept them first. Once you are at peace with the fact that intrusive thoughts simply happen and that you cannot really control them, explain them or eliminate them entirely, they become less distressing. Just try to view them as a glitch in your thought process and that they are not meant to be taken seriously.

The Art of Distraction

Distracting yourself from the intrusive thoughts can also be an efficient strategy. This doesn't mean that you will be pretending that they are not there, it just means that you choose to occupy your time with things other than mulling over these thoughts and therein lies your power. Engage your thoughts in something you find enjoyable. You could, for instance, try practicing a creative activity like pottery or playing a musical instrument. Perhaps you can also try hiking and enjoy nature while you are at it. You can even dedicate some time to read or watch calming videos on YouTube to take your mind off the distressing thoughts.

Exposure and response prevention:

Also known as ERP for short. It is a very efficient way to combat intrusive thoughts. ERP is a concept in which the human brain discards the things that it encounters frequently and views it as unimportant and meaningless.

You can use this approach by willingly and intentionally thinking about the thoughts that are similar to the upsetting intrusive thoughts that you usually get. Start by identifying the intrusive thought, maybe you often get the urge to punch random people on the street. Then, imagine yourself doing it. Picture yourself heading towards a stranger and punching them in the face. Imagine doing this about ten times per day and every time you do it, keep in mind that you don't actually want to commit this act of violence. After a while, your brain will file away this kind of thought as insignificant and thus unworthy of any emotional response and ends up ignoring it altogether.

Remember that the goal here is to solve problems not to create new ones. ERP is not meant to make you feel overwhelmed or distressed and though it would be normal to feel some discomfort at first, if it doesn't subside make a point to discuss these thoughts with a therapist and or simply abandon this approach altogether.

Spirituality:

Spiritual teachings and religions have addressed intrusive thoughts and though you may not be a practicing believer of religion, you can still benefit from its ideas.

In Islam, for instance, intrusive thoughts are viewed as whispers from the devil. These whispers are meant to mislead the human being, who is good by nature, and lead them to doubt their intentions. However, the knowledge that these thoughts are not your own allows you to discard them and even take pride in the fact that you resisted the evil suggestion. These are not your thoughts, to begin with, so there is no need for you to feel bad about them!

Medication:

Even though it is best left as a last resort remedy, medication can help reduce the frequency of intrusive thoughts and appease their impact on your mental health. If all fails, bring it up with your therapist and discuss the possibility of going on medication. Make sure you understand the effect this will have on your life and take time to weigh in the pros and cons before making your final decision.

Whatever you do, keep in mind that avoiding to manage intrusive thoughts or trying to control them by forcing your brain to stop having these thoughts may actually worsen the situation. Instead, face the problem head on. Acknowledge the presence of these thoughts and start applying the different solutions mentioned above.

Step 5: Identifying assumptions and core beliefs

We have previously established that flawed assumptions and core beliefs are the roots of dysfunctional automatic thoughts. After applying what you learned in the last chapters about identifying and challenging automatic thoughts, it is time to focus on what comes next in the Thought Hierarchy.

Recognizing Dysfunctional Assumptions

Assumptions along with conditional rules and attitudes form what is known as intermediate beliefs. They stem from core beliefs and have a big impact on automatic thoughts. They are mostly related to achievements, control, and acceptance. They are mainly what you think you should accomplish and how you believe you must be in order to be accepted. Thoughts like "If I were more beautiful, I would be more popular", "I should graduate top of my class to make sure I get a job" or "If I have more money, all my problems will be solved" are prime examples of intermediate beliefs. As those examples suggest, this set of beliefs can come in the form of unrealistic standards that put a lot of pressure on you and that are often impossible to reach.

To identify your assumptions, go over your list of automatic thoughts. If you notice a pattern, if those thoughts can be grouped under one common theme, that might be the assumption that lies beneath them. Assumption can also be in the form of if-then or should / must statements, so if any of the automatic thoughts you identified are such statements, they might be communicating dysfunctional assumptions.

Another way to go about it is to try and deduce your assumptions from the emotions that you are struggling with. For instance, if you are upset about a failed test, your assumptions maybe something like "If I don't pass this class, I'll fail at school" or "If I don't get straight

As, I won't graduate" and these are the type of assumptions that cause your anxiety about the test you score well in.

How to identify dysfunctional core beliefs

This level of thought encompasses both assumptions and automatic thoughts. It is a set of absolute beliefs that are even more inflexible than intermediate beliefs, they are usually basic and generalized and are relative to what you believe about yourself, other people and the world as a whole. As stated previously they are deeper than assumptions and they extend to all aspects of life. Core beliefs are not triggered by events and situations. They influence our perception and our understanding of what we perceive which means they also influence our assumptions, thoughts and eventually, the emotions that result from them. Much like assumptions and automatic thoughts, core beliefs can be dysfunctional or distorted.

Core beliefs are formed as early as childhood and they are honed and cemented as we grow older and go through life experiences such as traumatic events, living in a place that has seen political unrest or losing a loved one, for instance. As human beings, we are more likely to hold on to our core beliefs, accepting any evidence that validates and confirms them and discarding evidence that contradicts them. Though they have been strongly ingrained in our minds through the years, it is important to keep in mind that core beliefs are not facts. They are only ideas that may or may not be true regardless of how attached we are to them.

Examples of Widely-experienced Dysfunctional Core Beliefs

- I am useless
- I am lazy

- I am weak
- I am unhappy
- I will never be successful
- Money makes happiness
- There is no good left in the world
- Everything is pointless

Because core beliefs are the deepest level of thought, it would be a good idea to start by identifying your automatic thoughts and assumptions in order to identify them. You can also try to get to know yourself better and look thoroughly within yourself to identify them directly, but that may turn out to be a painful process.

If you choose to go through your automatic thoughts and assumptions first, go through the list that you have made of these thoughts and start looking for a common theme, a single idea that links them together. For instance, if you have noted assumptions like "If I make a lot of money, I will be happy" or "I will be happy if I get a nice job" the common core belief might be "I am unhappy" or "Money makes happiness".

Core beliefs may also be things that you believe are too evident to be stated or questioned in any way. So, think about the ideas that you think are too obvious and take note of them.

You can also ask yourself a few questions that are related to your perception like "How do I view myself?", "How do I see the world?" or "What is my perception of people?" and other questions that will help you shed more light on the issue like: "Am I worthy of affection?", "Am I a good person?", "Am I resilient?"

Another thing you can do is use the downward-arrow technique which is used by therapists. Start with an automatic thought that upsets you and ask yourself "What does this mean?" over and over again for each answer you come up with until you end up with the basic core belief that lies beneath that automatic thought.

For example, you can be anxious about speaking to your new boss.

> What does this mean? → I am anxious about talking to a new person.
>
> What does this mean? → I am afraid of their judgment.
>
> What does this mean? → I am afraid I will say something offensive or embarrassing.
>
> What does this mean? → I am incapable of basic communication.
>
> What does this mean? → I am useless.

Through this descendant approach, you have reached the core belief of " I am useless."

Identifying core beliefs is one part of the solution, the other part is challenging them and replacing them with new, positive and fair beliefs.

CHAPTER 5. CHALLENGING DYSFUNCTIONAL ASSUMPTIONS AND BELIEFS

We have already said that core beliefs are firmly set into our minds, sometimes they appear to be so natural and reasonable that we are not even aware they are there until we start the process of identifying them. This makes them harder to challenge than automatic thoughts and the process that addresses them takes more time. However, since core beliefs are where automatic thoughts originate from, you have to make sure you address them or else they will cause other new distorted automatic thoughts to form and all your efforts on the previous ones would have been for nothing.

To challenge core beliefs, you will be using the same thought journaling concept as you did before. List down the assumptions and core beliefs that the previously mentioned methods allow you to identify, and write down evidence for and against the core belief or assumption. Then, you can start examining each of them and objectively decide if they are reasonable or not.

Ask yourself if your core beliefs are reasonable, if they are true and if other people would have the same beliefs. It would also be helpful to ask yourself whether or not you can let go of that belief and how it would affect your life to do so.

You can also make a list of the most important aspects of your life, like work, family, friendships, financial stability, etc. And then, assess how your core belief is in each of those aspects. Take "I am unhappy" for instance, if you take a look at every aspect you listed, would you say you are unhappy in all of those aspects? Maybe you have a good job that you enjoy and are passionate about or perhaps your family is very supportive and loving, you may even have managed to balance your credit score and made the last payment on your student loans. If that's the case, can you really say that you are unhappy in your work or within your family? Does achieving financial stability make you feel unhappy? Clearly, the answer is no. This will lead you to reassess your core belief and you will realize that it is not true at all. Even if you are having difficulties with one of your friends, for instance, you can still derive happiness, contentment, and joy from the other aspects of your life. This approach will help you adjust your core beliefs in the span of a few weeks and it will help you improve the aspects of your life that you find lacking by identifying them and starting to address them.

If your core belief still remains firmly in place after you have tried doing what is mentioned above, try using "Behavioral experiments". This powerful technique requires you to hold a comparison between your dysfunctional core belief and another, more reasonable and healthier core belief that you would rather hold. You take one of your core beliefs, like "There is no good left in the world" and exchange it for another one like "These are rough times, but there is still some good left in the world" and pay attention to the signs that confirm this latter belief such as people helping each other out or feeding stray animals or raising funds for the less fortunate. Going about it like it's an experiment will help you distance yourself enough from your own beliefs and allow you to be objective and unbiased when examining core beliefs and assessing whether or not they are true. You may also have some difficulties and these experiments may result in evidence that will actually reinforce your dysfunctional core beliefs so it would be best if you do this with the guidance of a therapist.

Philosophy and spirituality to change dysfunctional core beliefs:

Core beliefs are the product of personal experiences, upbringing, circumstances, and culture. They are shaped by the concepts, teachings, and aspects we see all around us on a daily basis. This makes changing them quite difficult as every effort is thwarted by the constant exposition to what ingrained these beliefs in us in the first place. However, philosophy and spirituality can help you remold dysfunctional core beliefs into something healthier and more realistic.

While modern therapy as we know it didn't exist in ancient times, people still managed to take care of their mental health and state of mind relying on philosophy and spirituality. They allowed them to relieve their stress and deal with any upsetting events. In fact, you can benefit from them in this day and age as well. Philosophy and spirituality can help you by putting things into a different perspective and showing you the bigger picture. They both view hope, patience, and perseverance as key elements to a happy life and this will allow you to alter any unhealthy beliefs you may have. Using CBT and pairing it with spirituality can prove to be more efficient to you if you are religious and if you are not, you can pair it with Philosophy to broaden your horizons.

Patients are encouraged to meditate, pray and read scriptures and texts related to their situation. Engaging in group activities like group prayer, religious activities, charity work and the like can also help you by focusing your attention on other people and lifting some of the stress you feel towards yourself. However, if you believe that certain aspects may not be helpful for you, it may be best to approach them carefully. Keep in mind that many aspects of religions have been misinterpreted throughout the years, so if anything makes you feel uncomfortable, don't hesitate to look it up and seek a better understanding of it.

Step 6: The behavioral side of CBT

Behavioral activation

At the beginning of the book, we established the fact that Cognitive Behavioral Therapy addresses thought patterns as well as behaviors. We have already been through the cognitive side of CBT and talked about thoughts and their impact on emotions in detail, now it is time to focus on the behavioral side.

To start with, let's talk about behavioral activation. It is basically a strategy that will improve your mood and emotions by redirecting your behavioral patterns towards positive activities that you find enjoyable and uplifting. It is particularly helpful to people who suffer from depression or social anxiety and tend to limit their activity and isolate themselves. This type of isolation can potentially make things worse as it allows you to stay alone with your thoughts for long periods of time, reinforcing dysfunctional thought patterns and making them that much harder to break.

On another side, behavioral activation can increase your confidence and sense of belonging by making you engage in meaningful and helpful activities. An added benefit is the effect engaging in activities will have on your physical health.

So what kind of activities does behavioral activation include? The answer is a lot. You can do mundane everyday tasks like cleaning your house, taking care of your plants and paying your bills for instance. These may not be the most entertaining, but they sure make you feel productive. You can also go out with friends to concerts, sports games, art galleries or any type of cultural activity. Exercising at a gym, practicing sports or going for a morning run are also great examples.

In case you suffer from anxiety and have trouble with social activities, try to start with activities that reduce stress. Art or physical activities, for instance. Then, you can gradually work your way up to situations that now feel too daunting to get into. If you don't go out because you feel like you don't have enough energy or because you are not in the mood, just the act of leaving your house and doing something will make you feel better. You will get a sense of accomplishment and that will positively impact your mood even if you did not enjoy your outing.

The best thing to do when you are selecting an activity is to go with something that you enjoy, used to enjoy or think that you might enjoy. Spend more time doing things that you already do and that make you feel happy or try to include things that you enjoyed in the past but got out of the habit of doing. Exploring activities that you are curious about is also an excellent choice, so do not hesitate to explore new possibilities.

Service activities like volunteering at a pet shelter or a soup kitchen are great options as well. Not only will you find a sense of purpose and self-worth through such activities, but think of the impact you will have on the less fortunate souls out there.

If on some days you are not able to leave your house, doing your daily chores, as mentioned before, can give you a boost if only from the good feeling you will get out of getting things done and crossing checkboxes on your to-do list.

Here are some ideas that may help you:

Visiting friends and family.

- Learning a new language.
- Joining a book club.
- Trying out new restaurants and coffee shops.
- Getting a pet and spending time with it.
- Getting into a new sport.
- Redecorate your house.

After choosing the activity or activities that you would like to try, the next thing to do is work them into your schedule. At first, you might want to limit yourself to three activities at most so as to not overwhelm yourself. Then, once you are more comfortable or if you manage to have more time, you can add new things. Make sure that your new activities don't upset your daily routine or add any undue stress to you. Doing something for a small amount of time every day, or for a longer period once a week works well. For example, you may find out that the local music club has a weekly meeting every Saturday at 4 P.M and lasts for an hour and a half. You may also find that you would like to try gardening on Sunday afternoons. And so on. The most important part is starting, so make sure to note it on your calendar as soon as you can!

As you plan your activities, make a list of any potential hurdles you can come across and write down solutions that will allow you to overcome them. If you cannot go on a run because it is too hot outside, go to the gym and run on a treadmill instead. If you have a doctor's appointment on the day you planned to work on your drawing, take a small sketchpad and a pencil and do it when you're in the waiting area of the doctor's office. It would also be a good idea to think of ways that will encourage you to complete your activities like asking for a friend to keep you company or rewarding yourself with ordering dinner from your favorite pizzeria. Write it all down on a notepad.

Graded exposure

This is yet another strategy that aims to alter your behavioral patterns positively. Its goal is to help you overcome the activities that you find stressful by starting with something you are comfortable with and slowly making your way out of your comfort zone towards activities that you had trouble with at the beginning.

You might, for instance, be afraid of insects. You avoid sitting on the grass because of that fear and that keeps you from enjoying nature and experiencing the outside world to the fullest. You will need to list any activities that involve insects and assess the level of stress each of those activities trigger. Then start with the activity that makes you the least anxious. For example, you can watch YouTube videos about beekeeping or ant colonies. After that, you can go to museums and look at insect collections. Eventually, you might even be able to hold a ladybug or a grasshopper. Take your time with every activity and repeat it until you feel like it doesn't make you anxious anymore or at least until the level of anxiety is reduced by half before moving on to the next one.

Remember that this process is supposed to be gradual, so do not overwhelm yourself by starting with something distressing. It is also not supposed to be a traumatic experience. Make sure to take your time and be patient. If you need to, use music and work on your breathing to get yourself through the activity session. It is best to repeat the activity three to five times per week to see positive results.

Unhealthy coping mechanisms and how to change them

When faced with a difficult situation, human beings try to adapt to it by coming up with coping mechanisms that make life easier for them. Some of these mechanisms are useful and healthy, others can be damaging. For instance, when dealing with anxiety, exercising can be a good outlet for the nervous energy you are feeling. On the other hand, avoiding social situations, while helping you limit your exposure to stress-inducing interactions, can have a disastrous impact on your social life. CBT encourages you to hold on to the ways of coping that help you and have a positive impact on your mood and wellbeing. However, it aims to put an end to any behavior that may damage your quality of life both directly and indirectly. Bad coping mechanisms are a perfect instance of such behaviors.

Here are some examples of maladaptive coping mechanisms:

- Abused use of alcohol, narcotics or over the counter medication.
- Avoiding social interaction and challenging activities.
- Excessive sleep.

- Developing an eating disorder.
- Excessive partying and irresponsible sexual activities.

Usually, people tend to maintain harmful behaviors like substance abuse for the short-lived relief that they deliver from the anxiety that they struggle with. These unhealthy coping mechanisms only serve the purpose of distracting you from the stress you are feeling and do not have any real lasting benefit. Therefore, you must find out what type of "benefits" your mind believes these activities are providing. Perhaps they allow you to avoid situations you would rather not deal with or they provide a feeling of rush or pleasure. These behaviors are common and do not mean you are flawed as a person, but they must be addressed. Identifying the reason why you persist in these activities will allow you to identify the root problem from where they emerge and address the issue from its origins. Eventually, you will stop these behaviors and replace them with healthy alternatives. Furthermore, discontinuing them will allow you to face what makes you anxious and eventually realize that it is not as fearsome as you initially thought.

CONCLUSION

You have completed the book! Well done! I sincerely hope that you will make good use of everything that you have learned here.

So, you know now that CBT addresses both your thoughts and behavior. You have been made aware that your thoughts are divided into three levels: automatic thoughts, assumptions and core beliefs and you know that the upsetting thought pattern you experience originates from them. You are now better equipped on how to challenge these dysfunctional thought patterns, as well. You have also had the chance to get a better understanding of what intrusive thoughts are and how to go about dealing with them. You were taught how to redirect your behaviors and activities in a way that makes them healthier for you.

Remember to take it easy on yourself and to be patient. Do not be afraid to challenge yourself but be mindful of your well-being. If you need to, go slowly but surely. The CBT process is definitely not meant to worsen any condition you might be suffering from. I would like to stress the point of seeking help from a therapist only to determine whether or not CBT is the right choice for you.

Good luck!

One Last Thing...

If you enjoyed this book or found it useful, we would be very grateful if you posted a short review.

Your support really does make a difference and we read all the reviews personally. Your feedback will make this book even better.

Thanks again for your support!

Sources Cited

2017, www.psychologytoday.com/us/blog/the-magic-human-connection/201702/how-give-persuasive-speech. Accessed 12 Aug. 2019.

"5 Ways to Shift Your Dating Mindset." The Chopra Center. N.p., 03 Apr. 2019. Web. 18 Sept. 2019.

5 Mar. 2014, www.inc.com/sims-wyeth/how-to-capture-and-hold-audience-attention.html. Accessed 12 Aug. 2019.

"Amygdala." ScienceDaily, ScienceDaily, www.sciencedaily.com/terms/amygdala.htm. Accessed 18 Aug. 2019.

Careers Go to Grow. Work It Daily | Where Careers Go to Grow, 20 Mar. 2019. Web. 06 Sept. 2019.

Connors, Adam. "The Power of the Wingman: Choose Yours Wisely; Dominate Your Next

"Dating Advice for Introverts." Millennial Dating Coach. N.p., 05 Mar. 2019. Web. 20 Sept. 2019.

David, Tim. "How to Give a Persuasive Speech." Psychology Today, Sussex Publishers, 28 Feb.

Granneman, Jenn. "Introverts: The Complete Guide to Making Friends Who 'Get' You." IntrovertDear.com. N.p., 27 June 2018. Web. 19 Sept. 2019.

"How to Read Body Language - Revealing Secrets Behind Nonverbal Cues." Fremont College. N.p., 08 Mar. 2018. Web. 10 Sept. 2019.

LeMind, Anna. "Top 10 Most Common Human Fears and Phobias." Learning Mind. N.p., 08 Aug. 2019. Web. 16 Sept. 2019.

Jashinsky, Karen. "How Exercise Boosts Inner Strength & Confidence." Work It Daily | Where

Markway, Barbara. "Why Self-Confidence Is More Important Than You Think." Psychology Today. N.p., 20 Sept. 2018. Web. 4 Sept. 2019.

Markway, Barbara. "How to Keep a Thought Diary to Combat Anxiety." Psychology Today,

Morin, Amy. "12 Ways to Improve Social Skills and Make You Sociable Anytime." Lifehack, Lifehack, 27 June 2019, www.lifehack.org/articles/communication/12-ways-improve-social-skills-and-make-you-sociable-anytime.html. Accessed 14 Aug. 2019.

Parikh, Monica. "4 Truths to Change Your Mindset About Dating." Mindbodygreen. Mindbodygreen, 14 Aug. 2019. Web. 18 Sept. 2019.

Person. "Feeling Fine? Good Night's Sleep Could Be KEY to How Confident You Feel." Express.co.uk. Express.co.uk, 19 Dec. 2016. Web. 06 Sept. 2019.

Pittsburgh Better Times Team. "Senior Living." *Pittsburgh Better Times*, 4 June 2017, www.pittsburghbettertimes.com/social-setting-ice-breakers/. Accessed 21 Aug. 2019.

Quinn, Elizabeth. "How to Overcome Performance Anxiety in Sports with Psychology."

Richards, Thomas A. "What Is It Like to Live with Social Anxiety?" Social Anxiety Institute.N.p., n.d. Web. 4 Sept. 2019.

Schulz, Jodi. "Eye Contact: Don't Make These Mistakes." MSU Extension. N.p., 02 Oct. 2018. Web. 05 Sept. 2019.

"S.M.A.R.T. Goal Setting: SMART: Coaching Tools: YourCoach Gent." S.M.A.R.T. Goal Setting | SMART | Coaching Tools | YourCoach Gent. N.p., n.d. Web. 05 Sept. 2019.

Smith, Jacquelyn. "6 Easy Ways to Remember Someone's Name." Forbes. Forbes Magazine, 07 Apr. 2013. Web. 10 Sept. 2019.

Smith, Melinda. "Social Anxiety Disorder." HelpGuide.org, 13 June 2019, www.helpguide.org/articles/anxiety/social-anxiety-disorder.htm. Accessed 3 Sept. 2019.

Social Event!" NetWorkWise, 6 Mar. 2019, www.networkwise.com/the-power-of-the-wingman-choose-yours-wisely-dominate-your-next-social-event/. Accessed 23 Aug. 2019.

"Speechwriting." *Writing with Writers: Speech Writing - Tips from the Pros*, teacher.scholastic.com/writewit/speech/tips.htm. Accessed 12 Aug. 2019.

Steber, Carolyn. "11 Low-Key Date Ideas All Introverts Will Love." *Bustle*. N.p., 1 June 2018. Web. 19 Sept. 2019.

Sussex Publishers, 13 Apr. 2014, www.psychologytoday.com/us/blog/shyness-is-nice/201404/how-keep-thought-diary-combat-anxiety. Accessed 18 Aug. 2019.

"This Is How to Overcome Social Anxiety: 5 Powerful Tips Backed by Research." Barking Up The Wrong Tree, 23 Oct. 2016, www.bakadesuyo.com/2016/10/how-to-overcome-social-anxiety/. Accessed 13 Aug. 2019.

Verywell Fit, Verywell Fit, 24 June 2019, www.verywellfit.com/sports-psychology-for-performance-anxiety-3119436. Accessed 13 Aug. 2019.

Wagner, Kathryn Drury. "20 Affirmations for Public Speaking with Ease." *Spirituality & Health - The Soul | Body Connection*, 25 Apr. 2016, spiritualityhealth.com/articles/2016/04/25/20-affirmations-public-speaking-ease. Accessed 12 Aug. 2019.

Wyeth, Sims. “10 Ways to Keep an Audience Hanging on Your Every Word.” Inc.com, Inc.

Zawila, Steven. "How to Go on an Awesome First Date as an Introvert." IntrovertDear.com. N.p., 04 June 2018. Web. 20 Sept. 2019.

Made in the USA
Monee, IL
16 September 2021